RESILIENCE AND RESISTANCE

BUILDING SUSTAINABLE COMMUNITIES FOR A POST OIL AGE

RESILIENCE AND RESISTANCE

BUILDING SUSTAINABLE
COMMUNITIES
FOR A
POST OIL AGE

Tim Stevenson

GREEN WRITERS PRESS

Brattleboro, Vermont

Printed in the United States

10 9 8 7 6 5 4 3 2 1

Many of these essays first appeared in the Brattleboro *Reformer*, as part of our series
of monthly columns entitled, "Building Sustainable Communities." Others appeared
in the pages of *VTDigger* and *The Commons* of Brattleboro, Vermont

I wish to acknowledge and express my gratitude to the following people for
permission to reprint edited versions of their contributions to the "Building
Sustainable Communities" column: "Who's at the Table?" by Richard and Angela
Berkfield; "The Neighborhood Market: Local Food for Local People" by Richard
Berkfield; and "Farmers Markets: Affordable and Healthy Food" by Sherry Maher.

Green Writers Press is a Vermont-based publisher whose mission is to spread a message
of hope and renewal through the words and images we publish. Throughout we will
adhere to our commitment to preserving and protecting the natural resources of the
earth. To that end, a percentage of our proceeds will be donated to the environmental
activist groups 350.org and Post Oil Solutions. Green Writers Press gratefully
acknowledges support from individual donors, friends, and readers to help support the
environment and our publishing initiative.

Giving Voice to Writers & Artists Who Will Make the World a Better Place
Green Writers Press | Brattleboro, Vermont
www.greenwriterspress.com

ISBN: 978-0-9961357-8-8

FOR MORE INFORMATION, VISIT THE WEBSITE:
WWW.POSTOILSOLUTIONS.ORG

ACKNOWLEDGMENTS

In Recognition and Appreciation

THERE have been many people who have played a role in the evolution of the Post Oil Solutions community, and who are responsible for what the organization has become over the ten years of its existence. Without their involvement and participation in one way or another, Post Oil would never have accomplished what we have. It is with deepest gratitude, therefore, that I acknowledge at least those whom I recall; for those of you whom I have overlooked, I ask you to forgive an imperfect memory.

Carrie Abels, Taury Anderson, Becca Bailey, Janet Bailey, Jay Bailey, Angela Berkfield, Richard Berkfield, Larry Bloch, Lisa Marie Bloch, Dora Bouboulis, Chandra Bossard, Raven Burchard, Marilyn Chiarello, Dave Cohen, Anne Connor, Nancy Crompton, Jonathan "Slug" Crowell, Josh Davis, Steve Darrow, Marlene Everingham, Audrey Garfield, Amber Garrard, Steve Geller, Katherine Gillespie, Rebecca Golden, Russ Grabiec, Vern Grubinger, Kari Gypson, Gail Haines, Melissa Hall, Emma Hallowell, Paul Harlow, Cindy Hebbard, Cindy Hellmann-Flatt, Greg Hellmann-Flatt, Daniel Hoviss, Jeri Ann Jacobs, Patti Jacobs, Elizabeth Johnson, Liz Kenton, Sam Killmurray, Robert King, Meg Lucas, Megan Luce, Sarah Machtey, Denise Mason, Becca McMaster, Chris Martinson, Christine Meissner, Stacy Merrill,

ACKNOWLEDGMENTS

Jane Michaud, Travis Miller, Tad Montgomery, Todd Murchison, Frederick Noyes, Bill Pearson, Claude Pepin, Bert Picard, Lisa Pitcher, Treah Pichette, Mark Piepkorn, Louise Radar, George Reed Savory, Ben Riseman, Coni Richards, Deb Robinson, Leda Scheintaub, Barbi Schreiber, Janet Schwarz, Walter Schwarz, Liz Sheehan, Tom Simon, and Michael Whigham.

Most of all, I wish to express by love and appreciation
for my wife and partner
Sherry Maher
who has been essential to the project's success
from the very beginning

Contents

PROLOGUE

Opportunity and Post Oil Solutions   ix

WHAT IS TO BE DONE?   1

1. In the Spirit of Art Lettieri   13
2. The Fear of Inconvenience   17
3. Implicatory Denial   21
4. Post Climate March: Breaking the Silence   25
5. Intentionally Sustainable Communities   29
6. Climate Leadership   33
7. Power and Power-Over   37
8. Is a Class Society Sustainable?   41
9. Is Peak Oil Dead?   45

RIGHT RELATIONSHIP   49

10. Climate Change and the Growing Food Crisis   57
11. Building a Community-Based Food System   61
12. Who's at the Table?   69

13. The Neighborhood Market: Local Food
for Local People   73
14. Farmers Markets: Affordable
and Healthy Food   77
15. Toward a Community of Gardeners   81

ADAPTATION, RESISTANCE . . .OR BOTH?   87

16. Post Politics   95
17. Food Democracy: GMO-Labeling
and the Food Sovereignty Movement   99
18. Election 2012: The Politics
of Climate Silence   109
19. Resistance   113
20. Fracking and Vermonters   117
21. Climate Justice or "Climate Fascism"?   121
22. Hope Without Expectation   125
23. A Call for Climate Collaboration   129
24. We Can Do It. But Will We?   133

EPILOGUE
A Revolution of Everyday Life   137

Opportunity and Post Oil Solutions

THE Chinese character for "crisis" suggests that such a time is not only one of great risk and danger: it also presents us with a moment of great opportunity. Recognizing and acting upon this sense of fortuitous possibility is essential today, for it can empower us to create the sustainable communities we need to address the unprecedented crisis in which we find ourselves.

Unlike at any other time in our known history, humankind is faced with a climate-based mortal threat to our existence. Short of decisive remedial action and transformative change on our part, we appear to be headed for planetary catastrophe. As Rajendra Pachauri, the head of the United Nations Intergovernmental Panel on Climate Change, stated on the eve of the release of the IPCC's Fifth Assessment on climate change, "We have five minutes before midnight."

And while it is, perhaps, the most urgent of our challenges, climate change is but the eye of a perfect storm of crises that have gathered, including the demise of our democracy and the rise of the national-security, corporate state; the self-perpetuating, global war on terror; the class warfare being waged by the top 1% (and its allies) through the imposition of "free market" extremism and radical-right political ideology on the rest of us; the omnipresent specter of nuclear holocaust, whether as the result of warring nations or peaceful reactors; peak water; the growing food crisis; failed (and failing) states; and nations of refugees on the move. These are but some of the most dramatic instances of a world coming unstuck, in great turmoil, undergoing fundamental change.

And yet, it is within this increasingly fluid, seemingly chaotic context that an equally unprecedented opportunity exists. With so much of our global society in flux—with the old certitudes, institutions, and the only way of life we've ever known no longer viable, something we can still trust and take for granted—we have the opportunity to re-invent ourselves and our world, to live a truly civilized existence that is rooted in peace, social justice, and compassion for all living beings.

Indeed, we have no choice but to do so as a condition of our continuing existence. We live in a world where the chickens have come home to roost, and we must either finally do what we've needed to do for some time now, or succumb to our circumstances and their fatal consequences.

This is not a matter of making some technical adjustments to our economy, reforms to our political system, even changes in our energy sources (as important as that is!) so that life can continue as usual. No, it's a question of the values we choose to live by. We need to raise the level of our game to a new normal by being the people who, in our saner moments, we know we should be and want to be, and in fact have been at moments, when faced with an emergency or temporary crisis. As Hurricane Irene recently exemplified, we can rise to the occasion.

But now our circumstances necessitate that we be these people with far greater consistency. Our present situation requires that we be light on our feet, able to roll with the punches, unburdened with unnecessary baggage; that we be creative and imaginative, resilient and collaborative, generous and egalitarian. We no longer can afford the unwholesome behaviors that all too often stain daily life, nor can we any longer remain stuck in the adversarial, internecine power relationships of gender, class, race, sexuality, not to mention the original political arrangement of humans over the rest of nature, that have divided us from one another for millennia, and are at the heart of the crises that now threaten our lives.

If we're to navigate successfully the unstable and unpredictable times in which we live, we must make this paradigm shift as a condition of our continued existence. The old system no longer works; in order to transition to a more resilient, sustainable life, we need to do—and be—something different.

This challenge is intimidating, especially when viewed within the context of our busy lives and all that we have to do at present just to remain afloat. But what is seemingly "impractical" and "unrealistic" actually consists of behaviors with which most of us are familiar, like modest acts of human decency and selflessness, compassion and kindness, courage and integrity. We only need to act upon these more mindfully, and with greater consistency, with our families and friends, in our schools, workplaces, neighborhoods, and communities, for our everyday behaviors to be increasingly skillful and, hence, transformative.

And while, at times, this may involve stepping outside of our comfort zones, or engaging in risk-taking behaviors, we will experience evolutionary moments, organic to the directions we've chosen, natural responses to the growth we're already making. The changes we need to make in our lives—seemingly impossible at an earlier time—will become doable.

For by increasingly interacting with others in ways that speak to the best of us, we have a salutary influence on how we then go about living our lives in general. Healthy relationships, and the people they reflect, are crucial to creating the viable post-oil world we need and, in many ways, have wanted all along. Less driven by ego and the need to engage in all of those heartless behaviors that we employ in an effort to dominate and control the world, we thus are able to seize the opportunity before us and are empowered to live life in ways that support our desire to both survive and thrive.

In this way, we become the family activists, the neighborhood activists, the citizen activists—the everyday-people activists!—whom the world so dearly needs right now.

~

In the essays that follow, we illustrate how Post Oil Solutions has addressed this opportunity, the existence of which we have perceived from the time when we recognized the historically unprecedented threats to our existence: peak oil, global warming, and climate change. However imperfectly, this is perhaps best captured by our Mission Statement, which has called upon us *"to empower the people of the Central Connecticut River Valley bioregion to develop sustainable, collaborative, and socially just communities leading to a self-sufficient post petroleum society."*

At Post Oil Solutions, we have formulated four key components that will allow us to seize the moment of opportunity. They are **relocalization, empowerment, community building,** and **social justice**.

The need to **relocalize** our lives, and become increasingly community-sufficient around such basic needs as food, energy, transportation, and health care, is inherent in two fundamental facts: that we are at the end of the era of cheap, accessible fossil fuels; and that the burning of these fuels is the primary contributor to the climate change we're experiencing. What this means is that we can no longer count on the fossil-fuel-dependent, industrial civilization that we have taken for granted to feed, transport, heat and cool, cure, clothe, and entertain us and to provide for us all the stuff that we spend our lives consuming. This world is ending. We cannot depend on this way of life because the burning of the fossil fuels necessary to maintain such an existence is fatal to ourselves and other living beings. It is not sustainable. Rather, it devours itself, and us along with it, at the same time that it dazzles and addicts us to its technological brilliance, blinding us to our lemming-like direction.

If we don't make the necessary adjustments and adaptations, we will be left holding an empty bag.

We no longer have the luxury, for example, of trying to live the dream of a consumerist, middle-class society because that dream relies on cheap, abundant fossil fuels. That is its Achilles heel. Nearly everything about our former Vice President Dick Cheney's "non-negotiable" way of life, from large institutions to everyday minutiae, is completely dependent on fossil fuels.

We have but one choice: to relocalize ourselves. As families and neighborhoods, towns and regions, we increasingly need to do for ourselves what we have become largely dependent upon others—particularly transnational corporations and their political allies in the corporate state—to do for us over the past 150 years. It is important for us to recognize that these entities will be unable to furnish us with what they have provided us in the past and that, as a consequence, we'll be increasingly on our own. Hence, we need to become self- and community-sufficient people.

It is important to note, however, that, notwithstanding the serious challenges that such a change represents, a post-oil society could very well be one in which people finally locate the satisfaction and happiness in life that has otherwise eluded us. It will contain less material stuff and distraction, for one thing, and society will slow down to a less frenetic pace, providing more space and time for ourselves, with our families and neighbors, leading to relationships beyond Facebook and Twitter. No longer able to rely upon a fossil-fuel economy, there will be a greater emphasis upon attending to our basic needs of sustenance, empowerment, and community. Out of necessity, to begin with, but increasingly with that sense of purpose that makes life worth living, we will naturally become more responsible for the wellbeing of each other and ourselves.

Post Oil has largely focused on food in its relocalization efforts because of food's critical importance. The current industrial food system upon which we are so dependent for most of our diet is also totally dependent upon petroleum. As evidenced by the trucks and planes that haul our food several thousand miles to supermarkets with three- to five-day supplies, this is a very vulnerable system, one that can and will break down in the face of such severe climate events as droughts and storms, not to mention an increase in the cost of petroleum to keep it functioning.

Post Oil has largely applied itself to building a community-based food system to meet this challenge, as outlined in Part II. It is one that is envisioned as providing nutritious, safe, locally produced food that will be accessible and affordable to everyone, helping us to be increasingly food sufficient. Our goal is to help us become a people who can basically feed ourselves. Through the support of a vibrant, regional agricultural economy, made up of small and mid-range farmers and a decentralized infrastructure that will process, store, and transport their food, as well as the active participation of a citizenry that assumes increasing responsibility for growing its own food, we believe that we can provide for ourselves a sustainable and sustaining diet in these turbulent times of severe climatic conditions and dwindling energy resources.

When we begin to assume responsibility for ourselves in this way, to meet our basic needs, we **empower** ourselves. That is what it means to act on our lives rather than remain dependent upon and passive spectators to the corporate show. We engage proactively with our circumstances and increasingly taking care of ourselves, no longer viewing this task as the responsibility of someone else.

In order to transition successfully to the re-localized communities that are necessary for a viable post-oil world, we will have to both empower ourselves and, at the same time, support and encourage the empowerment of others, especially our children. Only in this way can we hope to meet the challenge of transforming our world into the healthy and habitable place that we've always wanted it to be and that we need it to be, now more than ever.

Though at first blush empowered human beings might appear to be the antithesis of what is required for realizing a third, key feature of a sustainable people, they actually are the *sine qua non* of a **resilient, collaborative community**. After all, when we think of powerful people, we typically see them as ego-driven, a quality that invariably results in a self-centered approach to the world that precludes the compassion, generosity, and kindness that are essential features in the communities we need at this point in time.

But empowered people turn out to be precisely the ones who make for a strong community simply by virtue of the fact that their relatively selfless state does not require them to seek and exercise power over others. On the contrary, because of their (relative) absence of ego, they are natural collaborators. Working together in non-hierarchical, egalitarian ways, sharing what there is to share, and deciding matters consensually—essential qualities of a sustainable community—are behaviors that come naturally to empowered people. Relationship-building, which is the essence of a resilient community, should not be performed out of some hidden agenda that is intended to advance one's political position at the expense of another. Rather, while undertaken with a clear sense that a strong, civic community is in the best *self*-interest of all, and that this is only achieved when people leave their egos at the door, relationships are built for the sheer satisfaction and pleasure the resulting community affords us, personally, when we follow through with commensurate interactions.

A sustainable community is a dance of empowered people. It is what a democratic society is all about.

But to be truly sustainable, a community must be **socially just**, as well. We all have to be present, to be at the table. No longer can we afford to be a society of the privileged few and of the many who suffer as a consequence of the privileges of the few. This is the heart of the brittle, very insecure and dangerous—not to mention, unsustainable—model we must evolve away from if we are to successfully transition into a post-oil world. As our present situation clearly illustrates, a society is not sustainable unless it meets the basic needs of everyone. This is what distinguishes the privatized, individualistic "communities" of post-industrial society from the ones that we require for a post-oil age where community is first, rooted in the responsibility for the wellbeing of all of its individuals.

In order to do this, however, the effort cannot be left to good intentions alone. These are fine, of course, and hopefully will serve as the inspiration for right effort. But because of the millennia-long habituation to such power-relationships as those based on gender, class, and race, we must close the gap between our good intentions and subsequent behaviors with a social practice that has the level of mindfulness and consistency necessary to make real what our words insist we want to do. We have to approach social justice intentionally, committing ourselves to purposeful action (e.g., Post Oil Solutions has a policy that any project it initiates has to demonstrate that it serves everyone, not just those whose class or race allows them to access its benefits). Only then can we hope to create communities that are both sustainable and resilient.

The breaking down of our civilization, along with the old order of power arrangements that have served as its foundation, offers unprecedented opportunities to refashion ourselves into socially just people. Once we allow ourselves to discard these ancient relationships like so much old skin, we are able to move on to healthier ones. We empower ourselves when we no longer require power over another living being in order to function in this world.

PART I

What Is
to Be Done?

CLIMATE CHANGE, and the larger energy crisis that it underscores, are no longer just potential scenarios for our children and grandchildren. Though their lives are, indeed, at great risk, we know now that the historically unprecedented threat to our common future is something that is occurring now and will continue to occur during their lifetimes, as well. As the growing legion of personal experiences and scientific evidence plainly attest, the crisis is here right now.

We are faced with the depletion of many non-renewable resources—most especially fossil fuels—that are essential to our way of life. Conventional oil production flat lined globally at approximately 85 million barrels per day in 2005. (The International Energy Agency estimated that the major fields will lose two-thirds of their production over the next twenty-five years, with their net output dropping from 68 million barrels per day [mbd] to 26 mbd by 2035.) This stagnation occurred in the larger context of the housing bubble burst, the financial crisis, and the Great Recession that followed in 2008.

⌒

But with higher energy prices, petroleum companies became awash in the capital they required to engage in previously prohibitively expensive exploration and drilling. Though conventional sources were rapidly becoming depleted, unconventional opportunities, such as the Alberta tar sands, Venezuelan heavy oil, natural gas from hydraulic fracturing and deep-water drilling, opened up. This has led to the black-gold rush of the last few years, where Big Oil has pursued trillions of dollars in potential profits, while they and their allies have jubilantly proclaimed the end of peak oil. Unconventional petroleum is rapidly becoming our main energy source. According to the IEA, worldwide investment in new fossil-fuel extraction, which will be increasingly devoted to oil and gas from unconventional source, will total an estimated $22.87 trillion between 2012 and 2035, while investment in renewable energy sources will amount to only $7.32 trillion. (Of course, this estimate was made before the glut in petroleum that has occurred in the last two years has driven down the price of a barrel of oil, making its production less profitable, and hence reducing its exploration and extraction.)

But what was seemingly a bonanza for Big Oil was at the same time a veritable disaster for the rest of us, as Bill McKibben made abundantly clear in his landmark 19 July, 2012 *Rolling Stone* article, "Global Warming's Terrifying New Math." McKibben wrote about three numbers that, together, starkly demonstrate that we cannot afford to burn these unconventional fossil fuels. The first number is 2° Celsius, what McKibben called "the bottomest of bottom lines." This is the increase in global temperature over its pre-industrial levels that the 2009 Copenhagen climate conference formally recognized that humanity must stay beneath if we are to avoid climate calamity. However, many in the scientific community agree with Thomas Lovejoy, once the World Bank's chief biodiversity adviser, who stated that "If we're seeing what we're seeing today at 0.8 degrees Celsius [rise in temperature], two degrees is simply too much." Our current trajectory is leading us toward four or six, possibly eight or ten degrees Celsius, which would be a potentially civilization-threatening disaster.

The second number is 565 gigatons, which scientists believe is the amount of greenhouse gases (GHG), particularly carbon dioxide, methane and nitrous oxide, that human beings can pour into the atmosphere by mid-century and still have some reasonable hope of staying below two degrees. ("'Reasonable,' in this case," notes McKibben, "means four chances in five, or somewhat worse odds than playing Russian roulette with a six-shooter.")

The final number, 2,795 gigatons, describes the amount of GHG already contained in the proven coal and oil and gas reserves of the fossil-fuel companies, and is the amount we're currently planning to burn, a number that is five times higher than 565.

Quite simply, if we are to cut greenhouse emissions by at least 80% below 1990 levels by 2050—which the consensus of the international scientific community believes we need to do in order to avoid rising above two degrees Celsius and, therefore, avoid complete disaster—four-fifths of known fossil-fuel reserves must stay in the ground.

Not only is the scientific evidence about global warming convincing to any reasonable person, what is especially alarming is that every measurement parameter that the United Nations Intergovernmental Panel on Climate Change (IPCC) tracks is worse than the upper end of their forecasts. Over the past decade, carbon emissions have risen way beyond the levels about which the IPCC has warned us. The heat we've caused has triggered a series of ominous feedback loops, so that the Arctic sea ice that previously reflected sunrays back into space has now melted, allowing the ocean to absorb these rays. And the immense quantities of deadly methane gas that had been frozen in the Russian tundra and the icy clathrates beneath the sea are now being released. Additionally, scientists believe that global warming is responsible, at least in part, for the vast dust-bowls in Africa and Asia and extreme droughts from Australia to our own Southwest, the acidification of the oceans and the collapsing of global fisheries, the increased incidence of catastrophic weather events and rising sea levels, and the growing food crisis being experienced by people in the "developing" world who are least responsible for global warming.

A recent study by *Environmental Research Letters* found that "3-sigma" heat wave events, in which climates are warmed to three times their normal temperature for over three weeks in a row, have been on the rise since the 1950s and today cover approximately five percent of the earth's land surface. The study concluded that "No amount of emissions mitigation can stop this frequency from doubling by the year 2020 and quadrupling by 2040, and by the latter year, extreme heat events will cover 20 percent of the globe. Furthermore, 5-sigma events, which do not occur presently, are expected to ravage 3 percent of the world's surface by 2040."

The issue, therefore, is not simply whether we as a species will act in time to avoid climate catastrophe, as imperative as that obviously is, and will vigorously develop non-fossil-fuel alternatives to allow us to successfully transition to a post-petroleum society. Rather, with all the carbon pollution that's already in the pipeline, as well as all that we continue to emit every single day, the question is also how we will adapt to our unavoidable, changing circumstances.

In short, we need to set a course of action by which we learn to live with that which cannot be avoided while mitigating our burning of fossil fuel so that we, and our descendants, can survive in some reasonable fashion.

⸻

The purpose of the essays that follow is to suggest ways that we can both adapt to, and transition into, a post-petroleum world, as well as to address effectively the urgent matter of drastically reducing our burning of fossil fuels. The good news is that we're not starting from square one. In many ways, and especially through the efforts of such groups as Post Oil Solutions and the Transition Town movement, we are already working to help make our families, communities, and regions more sustainable and resilient for the new world that we've already entered. An example of this work is found in the local food movement and the growth of a community-based food system that is increasingly allowing us to become a people who can feed our neighbors and ourselves by our own means.

At the same time, a growing nationwide and international grassroots movement has emerged—in significant part through the work of 350.org—that is engaging in nonviolent, direct action to oppose Big Oil's reckless pursuit of profits at the expense of the planet and all of its inhabitants. As noted in the "Resistance" essay, "From blocking the Keystone XL pipeline and hydrofracking wells around the country and closing dozens of new coal plants to fighting for fossil-fuel divestment on college campuses, as well as in several city governments and religious denominations, there's a growing movement of citizens who are saying, 'No, we can't afford to burn this stuff.'"

The issue, therefore, is one of degree; it is not so much an issue of radically departing from our present way of life (as good as that might be for any of us who are in a position to do so!) as it is of raising the bar of what we're doing right now, so that we are increasingly living our lives in sync with reality. This may at times take us out of our everyday comfort zone, introducing us as it necessarily will to behaviors and actions that are commensurate with a growing awareness of the climate crisis and the unprecedented transformation involved in a post-fossil-fuel world.

It's important to keep in mind that, though we may not be the majority of the people at this moment, what drives social change—especially in its earlier stages—is not necessarily a broad-based movement. Rather, it's the product of a committed minority, as the recent civil rights, feminist, gay rights, and anti-Vietnam War movements have demonstrated. Scientists at Rensselaer Polytechnic Institute recently completed a study in which they found that "the tipping point where a minority belief becomes the majority opinion is around 10 percent. Once that number grows above 10 percent, the idea (of the minority) grows like wildfire." As Margaret Mead famously observed, "Never doubt that a small group of thoughtful, committed citizens can change the world; indeed, it's the only thing that ever has."

This suggests that we need to be a more visible and vocal presence about the growing crisis. This includes not just letters to the editor and attendance at demonstrations, but speaking up with family, neighbors, work- and schoolmates, fellow parishioners, and friends of all kinds. Often we censor ourselves, fearing that we'll be perceived as cranks, when in fact those with whom we regularly associate can be affected positively by a non-judgmental, deeply-felt statement about the world into which we are moving. Yes, "dooming and glooming" is a big turn off, and should be avoided, but silence in the face of a growing disaster is worse yet. We've got to become a more public presence, emphasizing not only the growing climate crisis, but also the pro-active steps we can take to both adapt to as well mitigate climate change, that shifts the discussion in our favor by working together. Though a minority, this greater visibility brings attention to our legitimate concerns so that our concerns begin to enter people's perception of what's normal.

What lends credibility to our words, of course, is being seen by others as "walking the talk." Beyond words, our behaviors and what we actually do can give living expression to what we stand for. The importance that we attribute to community, for example, is lent credibility by our willingness to collaborate and partner with our neighbors, our non-judgmental acceptance of others, and our personal integrity in our everyday interactions with people in the home, the school, and the workplace. The value we place upon sustainability is evidenced by the increasingly modest lifestyle we adopt, and the thoughtful way we approach seemingly mundane matters like shopping, transportation, and energy use. And the need to be "resilient" is visibly demonstrated through the steps we can take now, with our neighbors, as well as ourselves, to be better prepared—less baggage more flexibility for the coming changes about which we can only guess. In short, it's living life as if we've actually entered a world of climate change that, in fact, we have.

Not only do our actions give substance to our words, being real about our situation is essential for facing successfully those emergencies that will characterize climate change, energy descent, and economic turmoil. When such events occur, not only will we place ourselves at great personal risk if we have not prepared ourselves for such basics as food, water, home heating, transportation, and health care, we will also be too consumed with our own problems to be of any help to one another. A community breaks down when its individual members are unprepared, scrambling to survive. Successful community building is contingent not only upon each of us being able to take care of ourselves so that we are in a position to help each other, but for the community as a whole to be prepared as a community.

Beyond actions and behaviors that help to build sustainable, resilient communities, we also need to be active in the political arena. As problematic as this is, given that the adversarial character of politics runs contrary to the consensual, collaborative, non-hierarchical paradigm that our shifting global circumstances demand, we nevertheless must build a political presence that forces Washington to implement policies that are in the best interest of everyone. To put the matter baldly, unless the corporate state becomes less corporate and truly representative of the rest of us, our efforts to successfully transition from fossil fuels to a society increasingly powered by renewable energy will be fatally compromised.

The facts are apparent. The technology for this transition exists, and continues to advance. Not only would an Apollo-like energy project exponentially increase our chances at making a transition to a sustainable society, it would also create jobs and spur economic development in the process. At the heart of such an effort would be a sensible policy that would remove subsidies for fossil fuels and, instead, add a flat tax on greenhouse-gas emissions, with 100% of the money collected from fossil fuel companies to be distributed to the public in the form of rebates for the increased energy costs caused by the tax, as well as subsidies for green energy alternatives.

⌒

What we lack is the political will to pull the trigger, to take the leap into what is already our brave new world. The reasons for this are not hard to discern. Using a legion of lobbyists (which, in 2009 alone, spent a record of $154 million to advance their agendas with government officials) and generous donations to political candidates and officeholders, Big Oil has been able to implement a stranglehold on Washington. In addition, it has funded climate-denial front groups, which, in turn, have generated stories in the corporate-owned media that create doubt and confusion in the public mind about the validity of climate change and oppose progressive clean energy and climate policy. (The billionaire oilmen, David and Charles Koch, for example, have quietly contributed $67 million to such groups, and plan to spend nearly $900 million in the 2016 campaigns.)

But the failure to act decisively cannot be laid exclusively at the feet of politicians and corporations. This is a societal disconnect, one that is both pervasive and profound, afflicting even some of us who have solar panels, hang our laundry on a clothesline, and bike to work. It's interesting, for example, that at the same time the clear and present danger outlined above has been unfolding, several polls have found a dramatic drop in the percentage of Americans concerned with climate change; while an increasing number of people believe that global warming is taking place because of human activity, they stated that it did not pose a serious threat to the public in their lifetimes: this is a danger especially for Vermonters, who, unlike our neighbors in California, for example, have been largely spared daily reminders of the ravages that global warming can cause.

While disheartening, this head-in-the-sand posture is also understandable. As the historically unprecedented transformation of our climate becomes increasingly recognized for what it is—the end of the way of life that we've always taken for granted—our interest in denying such drastic change has increased. This is perfectly normal human behavior. For most of us, it's only when our backs are against the wall and we no longer have any choice that we will finally act in the ways that we must. We humans, by nature, wait to do what we should do until the crisis is imminent: the "heart attack syndrome," when our situation is life-threatening, necessitating immediate emergency intervention. Then we act.

The question is whether this will be soon enough to avoid total catastrophe. There is a point of no return, where circumstances become irreversible, and what has been unfolding up to now in a seemingly tolerable manner will suddenly go beyond our ability to solve. Mother Nature, after all, does not follow a predictable, linear path, but acts both unexpectedly and exponentially in ways that can defy even the cleverest human efforts to exert control over her.

But our past history also tells us that we are capable of amazing things when faced with a crisis, and what seemed impossible can become our daily routine once we recognize the necessity of action. We are adaptable. Contrary to what former Vice President Dick Cheney insisted, the American way of life that is based on the burning of fossil fuels is, in fact, "negotiable."

The issue, therefore, is one of acknowledging and acting upon the awareness that the crisis is not down the road, something that we can postpone addressing until tomorrow, but is, in fact, here right now. We don't have the luxury of waiting until it hits us full bore; we must continue to do what we can to reduce our everyday dependency on fossil fuels while intentionally evolving toward a post-petroleum way of life. Even though we don't know how far-reaching the effects of this change will be, what we do today is nevertheless essential to a successful transition to this unknown world.

For by taking these first steps—by doing what we can now to adjust our society to address climate change—we are preparing ourselves, physically, mentally, and psychologically to deal with what we will be facing in the unfolding days ahead. As modest as these initial steps are, especially when viewed from the perspective of a larger transition, they are nevertheless the prerequisites of a sustainable society. If nothing else, we will no longer be stuck at square one; rather, we'll already be traveling on the road on which we need to be by the time we no longer have any choice.

CHAPTER 1

In the Spirit of Art Lettieri

Iwas reminded of the late Art Lettieri when I read the sobering news that **concentrations of carbon dioxide in the atmo-sphere had reached 400 parts per million (ppm) for the first time in human history**. This was a grim milestone that prompted one scientist to observe, "It means we are quickly losing the possibility of keeping the climate below what people thought were possibly tolerable thresholds."

Lettieri, a former school teacher, and well respected, civic minded resident of Westminster, Vermont, was operating his hot dog stand, "Art's Cart," one summer day years ago at his usual spot at the top of the alley by Candle in the Night in Brattleboro. Suddenly, he heard and recognized the ominous sound of an eighteen-wheeler losing its brakes as it came down High Street. Without a moment's hesitation, Art ran out into the intersection of High and Main, and successfully urged both pedestrians and vehicles to get out of harm's way. In so doing, he prevented what could have been a catastrophic event.

What Art did that day is precisely what all of us who are aware of and concerned about global warming and climate change need to be doing for our fellow citizens. We need to act in the face of imminent disaster; to engage our families, school- and work-mates, friends and neighbors about this unprecedented threat to our lives; and to encourage them to act accordingly.

On the surface, it would appear that this would not be a difficult task. After all, as one poll after another indicates, a majority of Americans accept what 97% of climate scientists are stating. The Earth is not only warming, but the primary cause of this warming is human beings, and which in turn is producing climate change that is an imminent threat to our existence.

Yet so many of us who are aware of what's at stake remain quiet. Despite its life and death importance, we find climate change to be a very difficult and uncomfortable matter to talk about. Perhaps this is because it is a matter of life and death: as a culture, we typically shy away from anything that brings attention to our always impending demise.

But there's also a matter of feeling intimidated. We don't want to be seen as alarmists or extremists, someone who's not rationally grounded, thus avoided by others, as a consequence. So we tend not to speak up, not to speak out about climate change. Ironically, at a time when the climate crisis has grown worse, and the scientific and our own experiential evidence about climate change is undeniable, many of us are silent. Knowing but not acting as if we know is another form of denial, one that us "non-deniers" can fall prey to.

As these remarks suggest, there are good reasons for our silence. But the fear of death and social rejection are greatly aided by a confusion that afflicts many people about the truth of climate change. This is evidenced in polls: while at least 70% of Americans believe there is climate change, this number drops markedly when it comes to the question of human causation.

Significant in perpetuating this confusion is the money and effort that Big Oil and its allies have poured into a propaganda campaign. Just as these same vested interests have shown no inclination about walking away from the potential trillions of dollars in profits they could realize from unconventional sources of petroleum, they actively foster doubt about climate change through using the denials of their hired scientists, much as the tobacco industry did about the link between smoking and cancer. Exploiting the tendency of people to want to believe that climate change is either not true, greatly exaggerated, or under control, this well-oiled campaign has exacerbated the challenge of speaking out.

The antidote to silence is not one of becoming gloom and doom in our relationships with others: that will drive most everyone away, for sure! We need to speak the truth, as we see it, but we need to do so in a way that will be better received. Timing and how we frame the issue count for a lot here.

Our challenge is to deal with climate change in a positive way, one that can inspire people to act while being real about the world in which we live. So we should avoid false hopes or platitudes about a better world coming (we don't know that); instead, we should offer ourselves: our concerns, our thoughts and feelings, and our willingness to do something about climate change. This is especially important. By engaging others candidly and compassionately, we bring to our discussion integrity, credibility, and a note of optimism and hope, the empowerment necessary for a reasonable and sustainable post-petroleum world.

There are no guarantees, of course, that our efforts will be immediately rewarded with the kind of results that we would like to see, but success here is not necessarily measured by the number of instant converts. Rather, the issue is about those of us who do accept climate change yet need to be engaging others regarding the urgent need to act. We can't wait for more personal impacts like Irene and Sandy to do this job for us. At some point, climate change will move beyond the capacity of human intervention to make any difference, and our efforts will be too late. In the spirit of Art Lettieri, we need to act now, at our own intersections of High and Main, sounding the alarm.

CHAPTER 2

The Fear
of Inconvenience

A T the beginning of "*Fresh*," an inspiring film about the
virtues of local food, a farmer relates how a Pakistani
college roommate once said to him: "Americans fear
only one thing: inconvenience."

Invariably, there is a reaction from the audience that I've
interpreted as a delicate nerve's being struck, a moment of recognition. We sense the truth of this observation. As lifetime members of the fossil-fuel civilization, we are steeped in a culture of
convenience.

Our industrial, highly scientific and technological, petroleum-
based civilization provides its members' relative freedom from
using physical labor to satisfy our basic needs—food, housing,
transportation, energy, and so on. This, of course, is in contrast
to the lifestyles of our ancestors, as well as of many people in the
world today. Petroleum feeds us, houses us, transports us, warms
and cools us, and provides us with the energy that makes the
"stuff" of our consumerist economy. Think of all the ways we get
around, for example, from one place to another; or the origin of
our supermarket diet; or that of the latest gizmo in our hands.

And how none of these things would be accessible if it weren't for the fossil fuels we take for granted.

A Canadian study calculated that one barrel of crude oil contains 1700 kilowatts of energy. With weekends and holidays off and a sensible, eight-hour day, it would require one person to spend 8.6 years on a bicycle (or treadmill) to produce the energy now stored in that one barrel. Given that the average Canadian expends 24.7 barrels of oil per year, every citizen of that country employs about 204 virtual slaves. That's much greater power than any Roman or Egyptian household ever commanded. It is equivalent to five times more labor than average the nineteenth-century U.S. plantation owners controlled.

Another study found that one 42-gallon barrel of oil equates to 25,000 hours of human labor (12.5 years all year long). The average American uses more than sixty barrels of oil equivalent (oil, gas and coal) per year, which suggests a fossil fuel "slave" subsidy of around 60-450 human years per person.

Work and energy go hand in hand; the more energy we can realize, the more work we can produce. Given its singular density, as well as being cheap and accessible, "sweet crude" has provided us with an energy source that is potent beyond our wildest dreams, one that allows today's middle class to live like the kings and queens of another time.

Yet if we're to survive as a species, we have to reduce our use of fossil fuels radically. We'll have to free ourselves increasingly from our "slave" labor, and transition to a way of life that, by today's standards, will be much less convenient. Successful adaptation to a post-petroleum world involves major changes, and nothing is more inconvenient in life than change itself. But when it entails abandoning the convenience we have taken for granted all our lives, it is even more challenging.

It's not that we must change immediately and totally from our current way of life to what we imagine a post-petroleum society will look like. That's unrealistic. Rather, it's a matter of moving in this direction by increasingly accepting the reality and implications of climate change as a fundamental part of our daily lives. We think about it; we talk about it with family and friends; we begin doing things by ourselves and with neighbors who help us adapt to this new reality. In this way, climate change increasingly can inform and reframe our everyday lives—from working for a living, paying the bills, and heating the house to driving to the mall, buying a new car, and flying somewhere for a vacation. We begin to rethink and alter our lives in ways we can live with.

As the most advanced petroleum civilization, America is also most vulnerable to its demise. The fuels that have paved the way for industrial civilization are responsible for destabilizing our climate. Accepting this fact is a crucial first step both to ensuring our survival and to living successfully in a world in flux. By seeing climate change as the new normal, and not as something we can deal with later, we begin to act in ways that are commensurate with what needs to be done right now.

This won't prevent climate change and its violent—even catastrophic—disruptions to our lives from occurring: it's way too late for that! We are already seeing the dire effects of climate change today. Nor will what we do now suffice for everything that we and our children and grandchildren will need to do in the years ahead. We don't know the future; we can only make informed choices about the present by being realistic about what we do know. Living more in sync with climate change, however, and acknowledging its gravity, allows us better to roll with the punches that are endemic to a post-petroleum world. We'll be doing, in short, what we'll increasingly have no choice but to do if we are to sustain our species on this planet.

With the end of convenience, life slows down. Less petroleum fueling our existence means less speed with which to tear through our lives in pursuit of the material comforts and endless distractions that a life of convenience offers. This, in turn, makes it possible for us to be more focused and purposeful, less scattered and mindless; we are able to both identify and give ourselves wholeheartedly to that which is truly important in our lives, a quality that is second to none for making a successful transition to the post-petroleum world.

While convenience may well cause our deaths, "inconvenience" is not the end of the world.

CHAPTER 3

Implicatory Denial

"We can feel and care intensely, yet remain silent."
—STANLEY COHEN

B EYOND the literal denial of climate change, another more insidious variation of this behavior has come to character-ize the American public's response to this unprecedented crisis. What distinguishes this from the original is that people are aware and concerned about climate change; they don't refute its existence and are disturbed by it. However, despite their accep-tance, they have normalized their awareness to the extent that they're not acting on it.

In her fascinating book, *Living in Denial: Climate Change, Emotions, and Everyday Life,* Kari Marie Norgaard terms this "implicatory denial," where despite knowing about climate change, most Americans respond to it "as no more than back-ground noise [to] the possibility that life as we know it will end." What is disowned here is not the fact of climate change, but rather "the psychological, political, or moral implications" that one would expect to follow from such awareness.

Public silence for the most part is not an absence or rejec-tion of the information, or even a lack of deep concern and car-ing. Rather, it's a failure to integrate this knowledge into our everyday lives and to transform it into social action. Awareness is not seen as carrying a moral imperative to act. This failure to respond appropriately, Ms. Norgaard claims, "flies in the face of basic assumptions regarding human behaviors that go back to the Enlightenment, and the origins of modern society."

Why is this? Why are we seemingly incapable of acting in the face of this existential threat to our continued existence?

There are a number of excellent reasons. At the top of the list is that "it's uncomfortable to think about changing our way of living in order to prevent something that's not immediately perceived as knocking on our door." Living in the bubble that we presently do, where climate change is seemingly something that is largely happening to other people in other places, it's challenging to wrap our heads around the profound changes that are involved beyond switching to solar panels and electric bikes.

There are also those of us who are not able to act because of a sense of helplessness and fear for the future. Many suffer an overwhelming guilt "for participating in a system that [we] do not know how to escape." There is no clear solution, and time is quickly running out. What so many of us are skeptical about is not the existence of climate change, but our ability to solve it. The antidote for both guilt and powerlessness is implicatory denial that allows us to not accept responsibility for what we know must be done.

This is compounded by the culture of individualism that pervades our society and disempowers people in the face of a crisis that requires actions on a societal and global scale. Norgaard observes that, unfortunately, "individualism is so pronounced in the United States as to create a crisis of civic membership" where we are unable to come together and work collaboratively around this common concern. This results in a loss of political power. People tend to see themselves as consumers rather than as citizens, and rely on "personal contributions to greenhouse gas reduction" rather than community building and social action.

All of this is exacerbated, of course, by the lack of confidence in our political system. Our alienation has grown particularly acute in recent years as it has become painfully obvious that ours is increasingly less a government of the people, and more one that serves the interests of a corporate oligarchy. As she correctly notes, "our current political economic structure is intimately embedded in our petroleum-based economy." Norgaard cites a Gallup Poll that indicated only 2 percent of the body politic feels they can trust Washington to do what is right. The fact that there don't appear to be any viable political options is critical to why we don't respond to this emergency.

Ultimately, the climate issue challenges our existing social order as nothing else has. Unless we can change our political and economic systems, "we are trapped." For our present system is incapable of embracing the massive social and economic changes necessary to address the climate crisis.

This is largely due to the class privilege that many Americans take for granted and the American way of life that has been deemed "non-negotiable." It is the consequence of a fatal anomaly where seemingly "intelligent, caring and basically decent individual people" can at the same time collectively produce a world of "such profound suffering, indifference and exploitation." How, she asks, "can 'good' individual people collectively generate such 'bad' social and ecological outcomes?"

Norgaard sees this as the product of a sense of innocence that is "obsessed with comfort, convenience, contentment, where the lights are always on," and invisibility where "the most intimate details of life from food, clothing or family vacations are directly, yet invisibly linked to the hardships and poverty of people in other parts of the world." As she reminds us, "Privileged people reproduce power relations as they enact denial in everyday life. We are protected from full knowledge of environmental (and many other social) problems by national borders, gated communities, segregated neighborhoods and [our] own fine-tuned yet unconscious practices of not noticing, looking the other way, and normalizing the disturbing information."

How do we break through this debilitating denial into active awareness, to act on "a new sense of integrity between self and world?" Quite simply, she asks, in light of the challenges we face, and the obstacles in our way to dealing effectively with them, "Can we make the path by walking it?"

Norgaard feels we can by working from the ground up. She writes about engaging communities in projects at the local level in which they assess climate impacts and develop solutions. In this way, people's life world can be potentially revitalized. This kind of effort "will reduce the gaps between abstract information and daily life" by demonstrating why the reality of climate change matters to them.

She states that "social movements around the world have emerged based on a fierce return to the local that may provide a key for breaking through climate denial." While yet to merge and be recognizable as one, the numerous civic, private, local and state groups that have developed serve as an antidote to government inaction. It allows people to move beyond that which has prevented them from acting on their better instincts and to respond, instead, to their inherent sense of concern and caring.

CHAPTER 4

Post Climate March: Breaking the Silence

"Hope is not about peace of mind. Hope is action.
Hope is doing something."
—CHRIS HEDGES

THE Peoples Climate March on September 21, 2014 was a great success, not only in terms of the amazing number of participants, but also because it demonstrated the climate movement's multiracial, class-diverse, and intergenerational potential. This is important. For while climate change is the paramount issue we have to resolve (or there won't be any other issues for us to worry about!), it's also the one that, at the same time, must include the other issues we face—peace, social and economic justice, citizen-based democracy, and an everyday-values transformation—as a necessary condition for its own successful resolution.

Those of us who went to New York did so to send a clear message to the world's political leaders about the need for immediate and decisive action around climate change. But that wasn't our only purpose. For if that moment of magnificent community is to continue live over time, it will be because we are able to translate the life-affirming energy that was loose in the streets of Manhattan that Sunday into intentional everyday efforts to successfully transition to a viable post-oil world.

What is to be done?

On the one hand, we need to become an increasingly resilient, community-sufficient people who can adapt to the climate change that is already here, and which will become increasingly part of our lives in the years ahead no matter what we do now. We can't avoid the consequences of the melting of the Arctic ice, the collapse of Antarctic ice sheets, the acidification of our oceans, the release of methane gas, and the phenomenon of climate lag, where the carbon that is being emitted today will not influence the planet untill 20 or 30 years from now, not to mention nature's capacity for exponential, nonlinear, tipping-point development. We've waited too long. Climate change is no longer just an issue for our grandchildren. It's something that we have to learn to live with now.

On the other hand, we must also become part of the growing international citizens' movement to create the political will to leave the oil beneath the soil, the gas under the grass, and the coal in the hole. Otherwise, our efforts to build sustainable communities will be for naught. The greed inherent to capitalism that values profit over people has now reached its inevitable end-game with climate change. Given the fact that we can't afford to burn the stuff anymore, the ultimate question is whether we the people will allow those special interests that want to extract the last drop of oil for their own financial gain to push us over the cliff of no return. Will we reclaim our power as living beings and assert our natural right, and that of the generations to follow, to simply live?

Whatever we do begins by talking with each other, bringing climate change out of the closet, and making it part of our everyday interactions with each other. We need to have community conversations in our homes, schools, and churches, in our work places, civic and fraternal organizations, and local governments, to discuss what climate change means to us, how we can anticipate its effects on our lives, and what we can do both to live with it, skillfully and wholesomely, as well as to mitigate its advance. As important as action is, conversation is the necessary prelude to the steps we must take. For talking involves a level of acknowledgment that doesn't exist before what is said is spoken out loud. By breaking the silence and treating climate change for the critical reality that it is, we're no longer stuck at square one. We're moving forward.

We need to engage our Select Boards, not to make them responsible for solving the mess we're in, because that responsibility falls to all us, but to encourage their leadership through the simple act of acknowledging the importance of climate change, and the need to do what we can to be as prepared as we can. Perhaps this could take the form of appointing a volunteer Citizens' Climate Committee. This body would examine what climate change means for our local businesses, public services, police and fire departments, education, food and water security, health and wellness, and transportation and energy, and then make periodic reports and recommendations to the town and Select Board. At the same time, it would help promote a culture that encourages the entire community to be involved in the effort to be the resilient, collaborative and socially just people we need to be in order to live successfully in a world of climate change. This kind of civic enterprise can only succeed, however, through the proactive leadership of those in such positions.

We also need to engage our neighbors with the intention of exploring what we can do together to help care for each other. Discussions of this kind will hopefully result in our acting collectively, perhaps organizing a neighborhood mutual aid group for the next Hurricane Irene, growing a neighborhood garden, or discovering the ways we can work with each other, right now. It's through shared activity and common purpose that we begin to learn what it means to be a true community, to work through the challenges of such an undertaking, and to discover its rewards.

As part of the effort to promote a community-wide climate-change conversation, Post Oil Solutions sponsors the Climate Change Café on the fourth Tuesday of each month (except for December), 6:00 p.m., Brooks Memorial Library, Brattleboro. In addition to films, presentations, and talks about climate change, these evenings feature conversations amongst the gathered as to what we, as citizens, can do for ourselves and our communities. While we encourage and celebrate the individual actions that people take to reduce their carbon footprint, we also recognize that the real effort that must be undertaken is collective in nature. Self-sufficiency alone won't do the job if it is not integrated into a larger effort of community-sufficiency. In a culture that has long worshiped individualism, learning to work together is challenging for Americans.

But it is only by coming together as families, neighborhoods, communities, towns, regions, and as a nation that we can hope to both successfully adapt to climate change and to make the necessary systemic changes that will allow us to transition away from fossil fuels to a more sustainable future.

CHAPTER 5

Intentionally Sustainable Community

I T'S too late to prevent climate change. No matter how fast we ultimately act to limit its potentially catastrophic impact—and we must act quickly or it will be too late to do even that—we have to face the reality that climate change is here and will continue to be an increasingly dominant presence in our lives in the days and years ahead. We can't avoid it or wish it away. Rather, it's something we're going to have to learn to live with.

This prospect is frightening, of course, something that can easily paralyze us into inaction, rendering us all too susceptible to escapism, denial, and passivity. Transitioning into a post-fossil-fuel world, and all that this might entail, is a mind-warping notion, especially for people like us who, at least for the moment, are blessed to live in a place where climate change is *seemingly* not an urgent, everyday concern. By now, Hurricane Irene has become a fading memory, no longer the in-your-face reminder of what climate change is all about.

Hence, to take action and be proactive about something when we don't yet feel our backs against the wall is challenging. But it's no less necessary. For when we do feel the wall it will likely be too late. To meet this unprecedented challenge successfully, we have to do now whatever we can to prepare for the consequences of climate change.

In this context, community is vital to adapting to the age of climate change. If a successful transition to a viable and sustainable post-petroleum world is to be accomplished—one that allows for a life worth living seven generations from now—then we'll need the lifeboat of community to negotiate this turbulent, unknown journey.

But let's be clear as to what we mean here: a post-oil community is one where a people are intentionally engaged with their neighbors through a daily practice of collaboration and generosity, compassion and acceptance, and who are increasingly self-, but most importantly, community-sufficient. We learn to take care of ourselves and meet our basic needs by valuing and attending to both the welfare of the other as well as our own well-being. Without this kind of social fabric, we're in big trouble.

Sustainable communities don't just happen spontaneously. This is so even in Vermont, where we pride ourselves on our sense of community; where ideally we can count on one another to step up to the plate in a moment of crisis, have our backs when that's needed, and volunteer time and energy in community efforts that allow our communities to be the civil places they can be. This is an invaluable culture to be living in, and certainly one that serves as the soil within which to grow what needs to be in place in order to live with climate change.

But it's not necessarily a sustainable community, at least, not in terms of the social relationships that we require for this brave new world we're entering. Despite the commendable behaviors we've demonstrated in times of emergency, the innate human potential for spontaneous, selfless behavior is finite. It has its limits, as we saw post-Irene, when the many examples of neighborly assistance waned in the face of the severity and duration of repairs and restoration that still had to be done. People moved on with their individual lives, returned to their routines as nuclear families, and resumed pursuing their individual activities as essentially private beings. In short, we came back to the familiar way of life that we had momentarily suspended, one that is basic to our oil-dependent, consumer-driven, industrial civilization. Community solidarity, while priceless, is difficult to maintain over the long haul within this inhospitable social environment.

This is important to keep in mind when we consider the kind of community we require in an age of climate change. Notwithstanding our potential, we are nevertheless a people who also privilege iPhones and Facebook over face-to-face interactions, where ego all too often trumps selflessness and community solidarity, and the cult of individualism is compounded by the drive to consume more. These are qualities that erode and undermine the necessary social fabric that makes possible the kind of long-term, community solidarity that we require at this time.

To deal successfully with our unprecedented situation that James Kunstler has aptly termed "The Long Emergency," we have to purposely create a mutual-aid culture that is woven into our daily existence, one that exists now, before the crisis overwhelms us, and that is not dependent upon spontaneous, episodic expressions.

Given this challenging context, how do we go about doing this? How do we forge the kind of community solidarity, the sense that we're all in this together and need one another if we're survive and flourish?

Once a community is able to increasingly commit itself to ways that work best for its members, and begins doing things together—from regular pot lucks and other social gatherings to practical activities like growing a garden together, making emergency preparations, or exploring ways we can share resources now—then the community has a chance of evolving into long-term, sustainable relationships. Two steps forward, one step backward . . . and several to one side or another. But the trick is to get to the point where we have this traction.

The issue is one of how do we begin.

There is no definitive answer as to how we can move beyond this initial hump of awkwardness and discomfort that will invariably be part of the process of a group of people's coming together to explore what a consciously-organized, mutual-aid association would look like. We will need to feel safe and valued in such a group.

I would suggest that some structure might be useful in the beginning. An initial gathering, for example, might include a screening of the fifty-six-minute film, *The Wisdom to Survive: Climate Change, Capitalism & Community,* followed by a conversation as to how participants feel about climate change. People could also undertake the four-session curriculum by the Northwest Earth Institute, *Changing by Degrees: Addressing the Climate Challenge,* where participants read each session's material (brief articles, book excerpts, and/or links to online content that are contained in an eighty-four-page manual) on their own before coming together to discuss them at a subsequent session. These might enable people to engage with one another to discuss an extraordinarily difficult subject and how they might collectively address it.

As someone who has had years of experience as a community organizer, I would be interested in working with those of you who would like assistance in co-facilitating such an undertaking.

Though seemingly modest in the context of the larger picture, the singular advantage of an intentional, mutual-aid community is that those of us so involved will no longer be stuck on square one as the crises unfolds. Rather, we increasingly will act as if climate change is present and real, and we are less likely to be caught by surprise, overwhelmed and blown away by circumstances.

Most of all, we'll be growing the resilient, long-term, life-affirming communities that will be the basis of a sustainable existence in the age of climate change.

CHAPTER 6

Climate Leadership

LEADERSHIP is essential to the success of almost any enterprise you can name. Its absence is invariably the cause of a project's failure. Governments big and small, work places, businesses, schools, churches, fraternal and civic organizations, sports teams, political groups, theatre companies, choruses, clubs, families, and just about all other gatherings of people whose purpose in coming together is to accomplish a common task all require leadership to be successful.

Furthermore, leadership is not inherently the "bad" thing that it appears to be; that is, it need not be the authoritarian, partisan, abusive, corrupt, and self-serving practice it all too often is. Rather, it can be enlightened, consensual, democratic, and *fair*. Ultimately the kind of leadership we have depends on the motives of the particular leaders and whether they lead in order to exercise power over others or to facilitate and inspire the empowerment of others. It is this latter variety of leadership that we desperately require at this time in our history.

Progressive leadership, particularly in politics, has been glaringly absent in the midst of the present climate crisis. True, there have been some municipalities and states that have been actively involved in preparing their constituents for climate change, but they are, unfortunately, the exception. And while these efforts are extremely important, as we'll discuss below, what they are able to do in terms of dramatically curtailing the burning of fossil fuels is nevertheless modest when compared to the clout that political leadership, as exercised through national and international policies and commitments, would accomplish.

I'm not confident that this will change in the near future: after all, the next UN climate summit isn't scheduled until the end of 2014 and whatever is agreed upon won't be implemented until 2020 (as if we have all the time in the world!). Furthermore, the current lineup of likely Presidential candidates for 2016 does not inspire optimism.

Rather, and this has been apparent for some time now, we're largely on our own, especially when it comes to adapting to the climate change that is already here and whose increasingly severe effects in the time ahead are unavoidable. As such, we increasingly need to look to ourselves and our neighbors, the people in our communities and regions, to realize what needs to be done and preparing ourselves as best we can.

Intentional communities are necessary to achieve the kind of social resilience we require to adapt successfully to climate change. That's one part of the equation. The other is local political leadership.

In this context, I want to focus on Brattleboro and specifically its offices of Town Manager and Select Board. I do so because the kind of leadership they can exercise is significant in helping the town and region to adapt to this life-altering world we've already entered.

Brattleboro is not just a town of 12,000 people, as noteworthy as that is in a state of only 625,000. It is also a regional center, the hub of southeastern Vermont, with the corridors of Routes 5, 9, and 30, and I-91 swelling its numbers daily with shoppers, culture consumers, and work commuters. It's a border town, with all that this suggests, a major and very accessible transit point for Boston and New York traffic.

Therefore, Brattleboro has influence far greater than the average municipality. This makes it a particularly important player in how our region prepares for climate change. It thrusts upon its local government the role of climate leader.

What does this involve? For one thing, it's certainly not the responsibility of these few men and women to prepare the rest of us for the climate crisis. That's something that all of us must do in our homes, neighborhoods, schools and workplaces. The nature of this unprecedented crisis requires nothing less.

Rather, the leadership we need from our elected and appointed officials is to publicly acknowledge that climate change is both real and present, and, thus, something for which we must prepare as best we can, before it overwhelms us. By taking this responsible position, our leaders can provide an important dimension of credibility and legitimacy to the issue of the climate crisis that is otherwise missing at the present time. Because of their singular stature within the community—because our officials are, in fact, viewed as the leaders—such a statement would make climate change *official*. It would impart a sense of importance to climate preparedness that both could compliment and, at the same time, elevate the efforts of citizens to come to terms with this phenomenon. In short, it would place climate change on the town's agenda.

But where might this leadership go from here? After all, the Select Board and Town Manager have many other things to attend to—matters that we want them to be addressing, as well—that doesn't allow them the time to attend to the details of climate preparedness. Nor do they have a pot of money to throw at this crisis.

My suggestion would be that, as a follow-up to their official recognition, the town leaders appoint a volunteer Citizen Climate Committee. Their responsibility would be to study climate change and its effects and then periodically to advise the Select Board and Town Manager (and in so doing, the general population) about the real and potential effects of climate change in our area, along with recommendations as to what the town might consider doing given its limited resources and fiscal constraints.

This Committee, for example, could examine the specific manifestations of climate change that current research indicates are likely to impact our region—from severe weather events to the influx of climate refugees, from new health threats to the impairment of public services, from a potential increase in crime to a potential decrease in food security, from the dislocation of box stores and national chains to opportunities for local entrepreneurs.

It could also sponsor films, talks, and presentations by authorities and experts in these specific areas, not only to help educate the public about the potential consequences of climate change, but most importantly, to make clear what communities can do to better prepare themselves through collective efforts. In so doing, it could serve what could be its most important function, the rallying and organization of the local population to address the importance of community self-sufficiency.

I am purposely broad-stroking here, believing that such a Committee has many possibilities, and that details are best left up to others to articulate and define. And certainly over time there will be specific matters that the Select Board and Town Manager may need to address or on which the public may want to spend money as the impact of the climate crisis becomes further clarified by the work of this Committee.

What I'm trying to suggest here is that with minimal, yet crucial, effort on their part, local political leaders could help generate a culture of climate preparedness among the citizenry. By implementing a Committee of this kind, local leaders could do this by mobilizing their most valuable resource, the good people of Brattleboro and the surrounding communities, to participate actively in a variety of ways to deal with the ultimate crisis of our time. By so doing, it would accomplish what effective leadership always does: empowering people to empower themselves.

CHAPTER 7

Power and Power-Over

As it is with so many things in life, power is the crucial issue when it comes to creating sustainable, resilient communities. Do we as a people have the wherewithal we need to successfully transition to a post-fossil fuel world in which we can both survive and thrive?

The answer to this question is especially important because it informs each and every one of us as to whether or not we can be effective actors, and how our participation and actions in such an endeavor can be successful. Do we, as average human beings going about our everyday lives in our homes and communities, schools and workplaces, possess the necessary power to make this transformation?

This is not an easy matter for us to address, especially as it's typically understood as a question not simply of power as such, of the existential empowerment necessary to sustaining life, but rather, of *power over* our circumstances, of exercising the force (economic, social, legal—or simply *raw, naked force*) sufficient to impose our will on life to the extent that we can be in control.

Down through the years, power has been viewed and practiced in a one-up/one-down, domination/subjugation configuration. This invariably has resulted in adversarial, exploitive, and abusive relationships that benefit one person at the expense of another. Power-*over* is the essence of political power, a zero-sum scenario that is at the core of the most basic relationships of western civilization: man over woman, white over black, rich over poor, and so on. Power-over is the way humans perceive the world, as evidenced by the original political relationship, us over the rest of nature, that began at least 10,000 years ago.

Unfortunately, it has also been the way that people have attempted to correct and change these unjust power relationships, by triumphing in the "us-versus–them" game. Notwithstanding our better instincts, the heartfelt expressions of compassion, generosity, forgiveness, reconciliation, and empathy that we have demonstrated that we're also capable of, human beings invariably conclude that, in order to cease being "one-down," one must become "one-up" instead. In a dualistic political world that represents power as either one or the other, we believe there is no other choice.

The irony, of course, is that we end up resorting to a variation of the same power dynamic that was at the heart of the original power-over conflict. True, the issue is now dressed up as "good guys versus bad guys," justice versus injustice, and freedom versus oppression. But these conceptions only blind us to what is really taking place in terms of the interpersonal dynamics. Regardless of the "revolutionary" or "liberating" language we employ, and the fact that the actors involved have changed places in the hierarchy, the ancient power-over dynamic continues, dooming us to yet another round of this endless, self-defeating cycle.

Nowhere is the world of politics-as-usual and its life-diminishing consequences more apparent than in the climate crisis that we face today. At its heart is the same quest for domination and control that has fatally compromised the better instincts of human beings all along. Since at least the dawn of agriculture, it is this highly exploitive and destructive, species-specific relationship that has brought us to the no-exit dilemma we face today. This is starkly illustrated in the mad pursuit of the very last drop of petroleum that Big Oil is seemingly determined to extract (and that the rest of us are allowing), through tar sands, fracking and deep water drilling.

If we are to transition successfully to resilient, sustainable communities, we must avoid this power arrangement in our efforts and evolve instead an alternative approach, one that provides us with a genuinely transformative strategy. We must do so despite the fact that our efforts to make this transition to a viable planet will be seriously opposed by those who profit from the continued extraction and burning of fossil fuels.

But contrary to conventional wisdom, political solutions invariably do not successfully resolve political problems; they are little more than variations of the political dynamic that is at the heart of the original problem. Yes, we must defend ourselves when our lives and wellbeing are threatened, as they are now by Big Oil and the corporate state, but this must be done, not by assuming an adversarial position in kind, attempting to triumph over the other, but by doing only what is necessary to render them harmless, to removing their threat to our existence. Hence, rather than viewing the defeat of our adversaries as the necessary prerequisite to the world we desire, our approach to them is one of disarming, restraining and pacifying so that we can all live together in a more peaceful, socially just way.

This can only be accomplished through the practice of the values that rest at the heart of our larger purpose—creating a society whose citizens live their lives and meet their needs by considering the wellbeing of the world around them, now and seven generations from now. We can do this not by trying to force others to conform to what we think they should be, but by actually living the vision of a sustainable existence that is founded on the acceptance of and compassion for all living beings, including those who oppose this vision.

Acting on our lives in this proactive manner is the essence of empowerment. It is the key that allows us, as a people, to be sustainable, community-sufficient, and peaceful. Not only do we increasingly meet our basic needs through our own means, rather than continuing to rely on those outside forces upon which we presently depend to feed us; to provide us with energy and transportation; and to educate, inform, and entertain us. Rather than simply opposing or fighting against Big Oil and their 1% allies, we live our lives in collaboration and cooperation with the rest of the world. An empowered citizenry behaves responsibly toward themselves and their neighbors, meeting the needs of both individuals and communities.

In short, we can act like the grown up people we sometimes are, and who we have the potential to be always.

CHAPTER 8

Is a Class Society
Sustainable?

ONTRARY to what many believe, we cannot extricate ourselves from the energy descent and climate change crisis
in which we find ourselves today simply through a technological fix. To follow such a course is to engage in the same
practice that got us into our present dilemma. As we're witnessing with the pursuit of unconventional petroleum, reliance upon
technology alone that is driven by an extractive mentality and the
corporate bottom line only digs us deeper into our grave.

Yes, tools, machines, and the technical skills and knowledge
that create and manipulate them is important to a successful
post-petroleum transition. Used wisely, and without the purpose
to rule and abuse Mother Nature, we can benefit from them in
the years ahead.

But as our industrial civilization so painfully demonstrates, a
society is not sustainable by its instruments alone. To use science
and technology, as we have over the years, to conquer nature,
ostensibly in the name of "human progress," but invariably at the
expense of other living beings (including ourselves), is the epit-
ome of an unsustainable existence. After all, tools are instruments

of power, and need to be treated as such, with all the humility and respect that such a responsibility commands. Tools can be beneficial when used mindfully; when employed unwisely, however, they become exploitive, destructive of the natural world, enriching some by oppressing others.

This question of technology and its uses goes to the heart of the biggest challenge we face in transitioning to a post-oil world. If we are to succeed, we must move beyond the power arrangements that characterize our present, unsustainable existence so these dynamics no longer corrupt and poison our relationships with one another and the rest of nature.

The end of human domination and exploitation is essential to a sustainable community. We cannot afford the luxury of the haves and have-nots (as if we ever could!), or the class warfare that results from such arrangements. A post-petroleum society requires trusting, collaborative, peaceful, compassionate relationships built on the essential interpersonal integrity of social justice. Fairness must pervade the body politic. Despite our human differences, no one is one-down to another. A basic respect informs all of our interactions.

We're all part of a sustainable society; we're all in this together. Noble sentiments and political correctness aside, a socially just community serves the self-interests of all because it allows us to survive in a reasonable fashion in a post-petroleum world. It provides us with the social cohesion and collective wisdom—the wherewithal of sustainability—required to transition successfully to this new and unknown world we're entering. In short, there is no such thing as a sustainable community that isn't, at the same time, a socially just one.

It is no coincidence that a perfect storm of economic, political, environmental and energy crises has gathered at the very time that class divisions are the most pronounced they've been in at least a century. As a statement from Vermont's Senator Bernie Sanders makes clear, the inequities in our society are jaw-dropping. The most recent study on income distribution, for example, showed that, "in 2010, 93 percent of all new income created in the previous year went to the top one percent, while the bottom 99 percent of people had the privilege of enjoying the remaining 7 percent." He goes on to point out, "Today, the wealthiest 400 individuals own more wealth than the bottom half of America: 150 million people."

The significance of this great disparity is underscored by research which has demonstrated that the degree of inequality among people, rather than the rate of poverty, is the greatest predictor of social ills in a society. It impacts life expectancy, obesity, incarceration rates, teenage pregnancy, mental health, levels of trust in a community, educational performance, and the status of women, with most of these indicators being three to ten times worse in more unequal societies. Even those at the top are better off in a society that is more equal!

So how do we build a socially just community? Is it enough simply to protest current class inequities, in the hope that our elected officials will do what's right?

While token reforms may result from such actions, it's dangerously naïve in this day and age to expect the political establishment and its corporate managers to put themselves out of business by creating a truly egalitarian society. After all, it's because of their power arrangement—they over us—that they enjoy the excessive privileges they do.

No, real change is up to us. A new government agency or elected official won't cut it; we need to do what needs to be done ourselves, by creating the egalitarian community we seek.

Fortunately, we're already moving in this direction. As the Occupy movement suggested, many people are awakening from the denial of class differences that historically has dominated our consciousness as to who we are as a people, and how we see ourselves as a nation. The unconscionable disparity between the top one percent and the rest of us finally is being acknowledged.

Now we need to take the next step and make intentional efforts in our communities to address the injustices based upon oppressive relationships. The assumptions and behaviors that inform our everyday interactions with each other surrounding class, race, and gender cannot be banished by good intentions alone. These must be coupled with deliberate, conscientious acts that help us develop a more socially just culture. Only in that way can we move from simply having the right sentiments and politically correct positions to more consistently doing the right thing. A sustainable society is a just society in action. Justice is not assumed; rather, we ask in all that we do, "Is everyone at the table?"

The payoff to this approach is enormous. For by addressing the inequities that currently render sustainability impossible for the marginalized members of our communities, we begin to implement sustainability for everyone. No more trickle-down; the new society arises from the ground up.

CHAPTER 9

Is Peak Oil Dead?

*"If we don't change our course, we'll end up
where we're headed."*
ANCIENT CHINESE PROVERB

FROM the deepest waters of the Gulf of Mexico to the prairies of North Dakota, and many places in between, the production of oil and gas in the United States has greatly increased over recent years through the industry's ability to access heretofore inaccessible and unaffordable "unconventional oil." These include the tar sands oil of Alberta, Canada, hydrofracked gas, and deep water drilling. Using new technology and financed by the rising price of oil during the first 10 years of the new century, national oil production rose from 4.95 million barrels per day (mb/d) to 5.7 million during the period 2009 to 2012. At that time, the Department of Energy projected 7 mb/d by 2020, while other experts claim production could eventually be ten million. By the second decade, the United States had surpassed Saudi Arabia as the world leader in oil production. (NOTE: Since this essay was written in June 2012, production has increasingly exceeded demand, resulting in a glut of petroleum. This has created a situation whereby, since 2014, oil prices have plummeted, and production has been scaled back.)

With this increased production, a growing number of people (especially from the oil industry, Wall Street, and the Republican Party) have loudly proclaimed the end of peak oil, dismissing it as a myth that has now been dispelled. "We're not running out of oil," they insist.

But peak oil is not about the end of oil. Geologically speaking, that will never happen, as the reality of unconventional fuels graphically demonstrates. Rather, peak oil is about the end of the cheap, abundant, easy-to-extract "sweet" crude (all of which is in contrast to the much more expensive to drill, more difficult to extract, and much dirtier unconventional energy sources) that has been the bedrock of our industrial civilization and the basis of the economic growth we've come to take for granted. This older oil still accounts for 75% of our daily consumption, but has been disappearing at the rate of three to four million barrels per day (mb/d) each year. As older fields dry up, newer ones that produce this conventional petroleum are not being discovered. In twenty years, cheap oil will be largely gone.

Given this development, peak oil is perhaps more accurately understood as a phenomenon where wordwide demand outstrips production. According to a report from the International Energy Agency (IEA), global oil demand was forecast to climb to 89.9 million barrels per day in 2012 (currently, the IEA estimates oil demand to be 77.8 mb/d in 2015 because of the gains in green energy, among other factors). Conventional oil production had flatlined at around eighty-five mb/d in 2005; producers could not increase production because new fields could not make up for the declining production from old fields, registering an aggregate decline of about five percent per year. When supply cannot meet demand, oil prices rise, along with the prices of everything else that is dependent upon oil, like our food.

But because of these higher oil prices, and the profits realized, as a consequence, energy companies were able to turn increasingly to unconventional sources, those previously identified reservoirs that were long considered inaccessible and prohibitively expensive, such as deep offshore oil deposits, Arctic oil, shale oil, and tar-sands oil.

Despite its apparent promise of a bright future, however, this shift to unconventional fossil fuels has a very dark side. For one thing, extraction and processing is extremely expensive. The Energy Returned on Energy Invested (EROEI) for the Bakken shale in North Dakota, for example, is 4:1, which means that, to produce four barrels of shale oil, it takes energy equivalent to one barrel of oil; this also does not account for the energy required to refine the oil extracted this way. The tar sands net energy in Alberta is 3:1. These compare unfavorably when compared with the halcyon days of cheap oil in the 1930 and 1940s—during which the EROEI ratio was 100:1. Historically, the US goes into a recession when we spend more than 4.6% of our GDP on oil, around $60 per barrel. In order to recoup their considerable investment, energy companies will have to charge triple-digit sums for a barrel of oil. Charles Hall, at the State University of New York, has calculated that it is not possible to run our complex civilization on net energy below a ratio of approximately 6:1.

Additionally, this bonanza is short-term. For example, the twenty-four billion barrels estimated to be trapped in US shale formations is only about nine months' worth of global consumption. Fracking wells typically don't keep producing for very long. While some have been able to yield as much as 1,000 barrels per day, the rate then falls off to 65% the first year, 35% during the second, and 15% during the third.

Then there is the environmental damage, like the deep-water drilling that was caused by the BP Gulf disaster in 2010. The drilling technique for tar sands and shale oil—hydraulic fracturing—uses large amounts of highly pressurized water, sand, and toxic chemicals to force oil and gas from the rock formations in which they are embedded. This has resulted in serious air pollution, wastewater problems, and concerns about the safety of water supplies, given the growing evidence that toxic fracking water is leaking into underground aquifers.

But the ultimate irony to this so-called "end of peak oil" scenario is the climate card, which inevitably comes into play. Again, in addition to its requiring expensive wells and causing environmental damage, there is also the fact that this new technology must burn great amounts of energy—and, hence, release millions of tons of greenhouse gases into the atmosphere—in order to extract additional fossil fuels to be burned. Unconventional oil and gas—the touted bridge to a fossil-free-energy future—is actually a gangplank to the destruction of the climate.

The US Energy Information Agency calculates that, barring serious changes, global emissions of carbon dioxide will rise 43% between 2008 and 2035, an increase that would eliminate any hope of avoiding the apocalyptic consequences of global warming.

Rather than allowing us to use resources, and the time we have left, to create a realistic transition to a post-petroleum world, this oil rush utilizing unconventional sources only exacerbates our addiction to oil and compounds our delusion that technology can somehow trump nature. It ignores the fact that the challenges we face around energy are essentially political, social, and spiritual. Our continuing failure to respond to these with vision and moral courage will only hurtle us yet closer to the edge of the climate cliff.

PART II

Right Relationship

THE highly technological, postindustrial, consumer-driven civilization that we presently take for granted is no longer viable because it's predicated upon the burning of fossil fuels, a practice which, unless immediately and greatly curtailed, threatens existential catastrophe. In this context, our choices are starkly simple: we can either continue to pursue our present oil-dependent existence and, hence, drive ourselves over the climate precipice, or embrace a transition to a viable, post-petroleum world.

In either case, however, a life based on oil is doomed, and with it, Dick Cheney's "non-negotiable" way of life. This is a non-negotiable condition of Mother Nature.

That our dilemma is both unprecedented and terrifying is evidenced by our widespread denial of, and inaction in the face of, imminent disaster. It's not that we are consciously selecting the option of suicide; it's more that, because we are so overwhelmed by the gravity of our situation and its implications for our lives, we cannot imagine a solution whose efficacy would be commensurate with the challenge we face. As a consequence, we allow ourselves to drift toward a fatal destiny.

What is to be done?

As daunting and unconventional as it appears at this moment, the option of transition is our only sane choice. In contrast to the way our species usually accepts change, however, it's one that we will have to intentionally and thoughtfully pursue. Historically, adaptation to new realities—especially of the comprehensive kind that will be required of us now—is not something we gracefully embrace. When humans change predictable routines and comfortable habits, it's usually because there is no longer a choice. And while this approach may work some of the time, this method only allows for change that will be too late to address climate change. We can't wait until we no longer have any choice, because by then the climate will have spiraled beyond the point where human agency can have a positive effect.

We need to transition now if we want to be prepared, literally, for tomorrow. We need to recognize that we have, in fact, arrived at the point at which we no longer have a choice. We've run out of time, as the world around us, loudly and clearly, is telling us every day.

⌒

What is interesting about our dire situation is that it also points the way to how a transition can be made successfully through the choice of sustainable communities. This is obvious when we look clearly at the world that is unfolding before us and at the perfect storm of crises that have gathered in recent years, both of which underscore a more general, societal breakdown. The world we created out of oil—the American Century—is unraveling, coming apart. Our petroleum addiction that, at an earlier time, dazzled us so much that we believed in a perpetual, consumerist Shangri-La, one we could count on forever, can no longer provide such an illusion.

One of the most significant paradigm shifts that must occur during this time of radical change is the move away from national and international institutions to regional and local communities, from the global economy to local economies, and from centralized political authority to more decentralized arrangements. Worldwide systems, like food, for example, as well as dominant entities like transnational corporations and the most powerful nation states on the planet are completely dependent upon petroleum to function and maintain their supremacy. These entities no longer will be able to exercise the same influence and dominance over the rest of us as oil becomes increasingly expensive. As time goes on, we'll have to rely more upon local and regional sources for the things that are most crucial to our wellbeing.

Out of necessity, therefore, our society will become re-localized. As a people, we are going to become smaller, less centralized, more dependent on our own efforts and resources, as well as those of our communities. We will not be able to rely on the global economy or Washington to take care of us the way we have relied upon them to do in the past. A life beyond petroleum will require that we become more self- and community-sufficient, reduce our scale of living to more modest dimensions, eliminate excess baggage and waste, and focus more on our basic needs and how to meet them sustainably. Out of necessity, if we wish to live in a viable human civilization, now and seven generations from now, we will need to become a community of collaborative, courageous and compassionate neighbors who come together for the common good.

Community is the necessary bridge from our petroleum-dependent civilization of the past 150 years to a society adapted to the world we're now entering. It's the way we can successfully transition from an existence in which we have allowed ourselves to become dependent on fossil fuels for our food, energy, transportation, housing, economy, health care, culture, and, yes, relationships with each other to a post-petroleum world in which we will be much more on our own, as a people, to meet our basic needs. It is through community that we will meet our basic needs, as human beings did before there were fossil fuels, now with the added benefit of whatever useful knowledge and wisdom we've picked up during the age of oil. Community is oil's replacement, the power source, if you will, that we need to assume greater responsibility for our lives, and to live in right relationship with the rest of the world.

⌒

A successful transition is not a matter of simply retooling our present civilization so that it can be a greener version of the growth-driven, consumer-dependent way of life to which we are currently attached. This is a system in which we no longer will be able to live and that we need to learn to live without, a system for which we must find a replacement. The middle class dream was only possible (at least, for some of us) as long as the cheap, easy-to-access, "sweet" crude kept coming out of the ground, and we remained in a state of consumer bliss and climate innocence. Those days are over.

Thus, more fundamental to a successful transition than simply replacing fossil fuels with green technology is how we employ these brilliant extensions of ourselves. After all, technology is neutral until it's put to use. If it continues to serve as a tool with which to dominate and control nature, to exploit and oppress our fellow human beings, the fact that it's "green" will make very little difference for a successful transition. To use green energy to power a fossil-fuel way of life, whose profit-making purpose revolves around the extraction of finite resources and perpetual growth, only sends us further down the road to collapse.

This is why transition is ultimately about a right relationship—with nature and ourselves—and its vital importance in producing a social fabric within which to sustain communities, even in the most trying and challenging times.

Right relationship should not be confused with what we've typically described as "politically correct." In contrast to the latter, right relationship does not consist of the deeming of behaviors to be "correct" or "right" (as opposed to "incorrect" or wrong"), but is founded on the acceptance of one another for the people we are. In this way, right relationship entails a quality of interaction that is free of judgments. It is characterized by compassion, generosity, and moral integrity, as opposed to arbitrary standards of behavior that one group attempts to impose upon others as "correct."

Being nonjudgmental is acting without ego and its need to divide our world into the dichotomous categories it creates in its efforts to manage the world. When we accept each other for the instance of life that we all are, we act without "I," our behaviors are not burdened by the baggage that invariably accompanies ego, and that is then projected onto the world through our species-specific practice of domination/submission toward the rest of life. As a consequence, our contact with others is cleaner: minus a political agenda, human interaction is more selfless and real. Without "I" getting in the way, our behavior is heartfelt, characterized by an integrity that allows a community of human beings to be truly sustainable and resilient.

Ultimately, right relationship is the practice of acting upon those values that support and sustain life. It bridges the gap between the contradiction between what we say we believe and the behavior for which we often settle. Right relationship links good intentions with actually doing the right thing. This is because of its essentially accepting nature, a quality that allows us to be in right relationship with both ourselves and the rest of life. It is the power we require to successfully transition from the world of oil and ego, to a life of true community beyond either.

CHAPTER 10

Climate Change
and the
Growing Food Crisis

*(NOTE: Though this essay was written about the drought
conditions, heat waves and food crisis in 2012, its relevance
to today is underscored by the extreme drought that our
neighbors in California are experiencing, and the threat that
this represents to a major source of the nation's food supply, as
well as the continuing food crisis in the Global South.)*

WITH its unprecedented heat waves, droughts, and wild-
fires, the summer of 2012 could be when Americans
begin to take seriously global warming, climate
change, and the much-related growing food crisis.

Consider the following: the National Climatic Data Center's
recently released "State of the Climate" report states that the
January–June period of 2012 was the warmest first half of any
year on record. Author Bill McKibben noted, in an August
Rolling Stone article, that June was the 327th consecutive month
in which global temperatures exceeded the twentieth-century
average. The odds that this would occur by simple chance, he

observed, "were 3.7 x 10^99, a number considerably larger than the number of stars in the universe."

In the Washington Post, dated August 5, 2012, NASA scientist James Hanson wrote that the analysis he and his colleagues have done shows that "there is virtually no explanation other than climate change for the extreme hot weather of the recent past." This is based on "actual observations of weather events and temperatures that have happened [and that] revealed a stunning increase in the frequency of hot summers."

According to a *New York Times* op-ed article from August 11, 2012, climate-model projections suggest that "a coming megadrought—a prolonged, multidecade period of significantly below-average precipitation—is possible and likely in the American West." Though they once were considered rare, "widespread annual droughts have become more frequent and are set to become the 'new normal.'"

As with other recent, devastating, climate-caused events in the world, this summer's killer heat waves and droughts are having a major impact on our agriculture. In July 2012, the USDA declared more than a thousand counties in 26 states to be natural disaster areas. According to the Agriculture Department, this year's corn yield is projected to be the lowest since 1995 because of damage from the nation's worst drought in 56 years. All of this means higher food costs in the months ahead as the prices of corn and other crops rise to record highs.

The world food crisis has been growing since 2008, simultaneously with rising oil prices: symbiotically entwined, the fate of one dictates the fate of the other. For many in the world, this has meant hunger, famine, and food riots; for us in America, they have entailed higher food prices and deprivation for many, especially impacting the growing number of income-challenged people in our society.

These folks are the canaries in the coal mine, the first to experience the adverse impact that climate change is having on food. But food insecurity will become an increasing concern for growing numbers of us as the Great Recession continues and food competes with other necessities for our shrinking disposable income.

In this context, is it not unreasonable to ask: how are we going to feed ourselves? It's not that famine and extreme hunger are as imminent for most of us as they are for others in the world; it's that we should not wait until they are to do something about food security. What are our options?

There's no reason to believe that corporate technology will save the day. Preliminary tests this summer from Monsanto, for example, indicate that their highly touted drought-resistant corn, a genetically modified organism (GMO), is likely to be of no value in severe to extreme drought conditions, and only of some help in moderate droughts.

Nor will industrial agriculture—our present food system—be of much assistance. Wedded as it is to chemicals (hence, petroleum) as the way to grow food, it's unprepared for drought conditions. Farming organically, instead, would retain more water and improve soil quality.

As for the politicians: when was the last time we heard any presidential hopefuls use the words, "climate change" or "food security" during a campaign?

And it's not likely we'll catch a break from Mother Nature, either. Even if we were to turn off the carbon spigot overnight, the earth is already committed to decades of warming because of all the greenhouse gases we've dumped into the atmosphere since the beginning of the Industrial Revolution. As James Hanson wrote, "the extremes are becoming much more frequent and intense."

No, it's up to the good citizenship of ordinary people to figure out how we're going to feed our neighbors and ourselves. It's up to you and me.

First steps, of course, include supporting our local and regional farmers by joining their CSAs (Community Supported Agriculture programs), visiting their farm stands in season, and shopping at the many farmers markets in the area. There are a number of retail outlets as well that carry locally produced, such as the Brattleboro and Putney Food Co-ops, and the River Bend Market in Townshend.

As we begin this task, we would do well to consider the example of our grandparents and great-grandparents, who grew their "Victory Gardens" during World War II as families and communities during another time of crisis. While supporting local agriculture is essential to our wellbeing, we also need to become communities of gardeners, people who take increasing responsibility for growing our food, and who, collaboratively, provide the basis of food security for all of us. Organizing community gardens, for example, is an invaluable way of bringing people together in a collective effort; along with the "Grow a Row" efforts of individual gardeners, they are especially important in providing food for local food shelves. Workshops that impart not only knowledge about growing our food, but also teach such skills as canning, root cellaring, and other ways of putting food by like seed saving, extending the season, and cooking with local food, are essential to becoming food sufficient, food secure.

Becoming a people who can feed ourselves and our neighbors is second to none, for increasingly evolving into the self-sufficient/community-sufficient people we need to be in order to successfully transition into a post-oil age.

CHAPTER 11

Building a Community-Based Food System

"I don't know why Windham County couldn't feed itself."
—PAUL HARLOW, *Westminster farmer, 24 October 2007, at the Windham Farm Bureau's forum, Local Agriculture and Global Warming*

NOTHING is more basic to creating resilient communities than the re-localization of our food system. Second only to having the water we require for sustaining life, we must be able to feed ourselves if we are to transition successfully into a post-petroleum world.

This need is underscored by the fact that our present diet is completely dependent on fossil fuels for its production and distribution. From seeds and fertilizer, herbicides and pesticides, irrigation and harvesting, to processing and packaging, refrigeration and transportation—in short, from field to table—our industrial, profit-driven, global food system could not exist without oil and gas.

This is especially problematic when we consider that the production of oil is becoming increasingly expensive. It was no coincidence, for example, that at the same time that conventional oil production peaked in 2005, causing such an increase in the price of oil that the cost of world food also rose. This led to the food crisis of 2008, which caused starvation and food riots in several countries. This problem is exacerbated by the advent of global warming and climate change. We need to move from the burning of fossil fuels as quickly as we can if we are to retain a livable planet.

Thus, in addition to other serious issues about our industrial food system, particularly the health, safety, and nutrition of its products, our current food system is not sustainable.

Even an agricultural state like Vermont is very dependent upon industrially produced food, which travels from 3,000 to 6,000 miles away, or farther. Though we lead the nation in per capita direct farm sales, we still import approximately 80% of our food. This extreme vulnerability to contingencies beyond our control is underscored by the fact that our average supermarket only has enough food on hand for three to five days. Unless we are a people who can feed ourselves through our own production and that of our local and regional farmers, our diet will continue to be at the mercy of global oil prices, long-term power outages, and transportation failures that could be caused by the kind of 100 year climate change-related weather events we're now experiencing with greater frequency.

Not surprisingly, Post Oil Solutions has made food and the building of a regional, community-based food system our top priority since our founding in 2005. We are part of larger movement, both in Vermont and throughout the country, that is practicing the "Three *Rs*"—**relocalization, resiliency and redundancy**—so that we can become self-sufficient and food-secure.

We started by launching a variety of modest projects, including three community gardens in Brattleboro, the Brattleboro Winter Farmers' Market, and the Townshend Common Farmers' Market, and our (Re)learning to Feed Ourselves workshop series. While raising awareness regarding the importance of local food and providing some community infrastructure that would allow people to better feed themselves, these efforts were most important in building relationships between members of the agricultural and greater, regional community, a need that we've always considered second to none for achieving our purpose.

One of our earliest endeavors was the Eat More Local Food campaign, in which over 1,000 people signed a pledge, later published in the *Brattleboro Reformer,* stating that they would include more local food in their daily diets. This evolved into our semi-annual summer and winter Localvore Challenges, in which people committed to eating food that was grown within a hundred-mile radius of Brattleboro.

While this effort was especially helpful in raising awareness about local food and making the word "localvore" a part of our everyday lexicon, it also introduced at least two important lessons that we needed to learn. The first of these was that, despite its success in encouraging people to eat more local food, we discovered that the localvore movement was not inclusive of the entire community. It overlooked the 12% of Vermonters who are struggling to put any food on the table and others who cannot access or afford local food. Despite the transportation costs of food from thousands of miles away, this expense was offset by the generous subsidies that industrial farmers received from the federal government, often allowing them to undersell local farmers. As a consequence, the local food movement was basically a white, middle-class phenomenon, peopled by those whose income and race allowed them to privilege local food. This revelation drew attention to our growing understanding that unless everyone was at the table, it rendered moot the realization of a sustainable community.

From this experience, we became much more intentional about social justice in our work and mission, addressing racial and class barriers in all of our projects, especially sourcing food. From holding retreats for ourselves around class and race, to making it a requirement that all our future projects purposely address the question of inclusion, we have evolved a richer, more equitable practice.

An early example of this was our Community Food Security Project (CFSP), which had the mission to "increase the access to locally produced food for all people regardless of income." Among its several efforts,

- it initiated and collaborated on a variety of projects, including several new community gardens;

- self-watering container garden projects with several partners, including the Southern Vermont AIDS Project;

- a partnership with the Vermont Food Bank to bring gleaning to Windham County that realized 95,000 pounds of produce from local farms in its first two years alone;

- the creation of a two-acre farm at School for International Training that, in part, provided food to Brattleboro's Drop-In Center;

- conducting a Rapid Community Food Assessment, which collected data as to what needed to be done to make the area more food-secure, that was outlined in the report of their findings and recommendations, "Healthy Food is a Human Right."

Following up on one of these recommendations, the CFSP began the Market Basket project in two lower-to-moderate-income neighborhoods. Now known as the Neighborhood Market, and located at the Green Street School in Brattleboro, this is a weekly farmers' market during the summer months that features wholesale prices from socially-conscious farmers for food-stamp-eligible customers, which accepts payment with EBT cards.

The second lesson that emerged from the localvore campaign came unexpectedly from the very people we intended to be helping: local and regional farmers. The increased interest in local food created a demand for which some farmers were both unprepared and not ready to meet. Hence, some farmers were not happy about this development. What we belatedly realized was that if we wanted our local and regional farmers to grow increasing amounts of food to provide for a growing need, the community had to help provide the necessary infrastructure and services. This was the genesis of the Great Falls Food Hub, a project that was originally an invaluable partnership with the South-Eastern Vermont Community Action Agency (SEVCA). It envisioned creating a large, multi-purpose commercial kitchen, dry-, cold-, and frozen-storage facilities, a distribution service, an incubator farm, and a variety of marketing services for farmers.

This goal has proven to be most challenging to realize, and hence, it remains a work in progress. However, a distribution service, the Windham Farm and Food Network (WFFN, now simply WFF) was independently organized and realized, and Post Oil has helped to manage it. WFF has now become part of Food Connects, which is mentioned below.

Another strategic effort was the creation of the Windham County Farm to School Program, an effort that was inspired by the understanding of the importance of making the next generation food-literate. The initial efforts and success were the result of the dedicated efforts of a core of Brattleboro schoolteachers. By collaborating with these people, Post Oil's Farm to School program helped to organize school gardens, taste-tests and farm visits for students; to introduce local farm food into schools' lunch programs (especially through the involvement of WFFN); and to provide teacher education and training using its annual Farm to School Conferences and series of workshops.

More recently, Buying Clubs have been initiated at a number of Brattleboro schools. Through weekly deliveries by WFF, people are able to access local farm food at wholesale prices.

Together with the Farm to School Program and the Neighborhood Market, the Buying Clubs became an independent project in 2013 under the umbrella name of Food Connects. This move reflects Post Oil's commitment to being a community organizing project whose purpose is to help start or support initiatives that eventually are able to stand on their own. Other examples of this have included the Townshend Common Farmers' market, the Windham Energy Group (now Southern Vermont Co-op Power), and Brattleboro Time Bank.

Crucial to building a community-based food system, however, is our reconnecting with our food and becoming more self-sufficient in obtaining our food. Not only do we need to reduce our dependency on the supermarket, we also cannot rely on our local farmers alone to feed us. We have to grow some of our own food as well, and we must learn to cultivate our gardens twelve months of the year by using cold frames, hoophouses, root cellars, and canning and other preservation efforts. And while our workshops are re-kindling this knowledge that our grandparents took for granted, we have also encouraged collaborative efforts— neighbors helping neighbors through our Neighborhood Garden Support network and our annual No Gardener Left Behind Expo that we hosted in our earlier years.

This approach, which is the fundamental step to creating a resilient and redundant, community-sufficient local food system, was the basis of the Food Security Collaborative (formerly the Greater Falls Community Garden Collaborative). This initiative grew out of community conversations that Post Oil sponsored in the Bellows Falls area. Although it has ceased to exist as a project of Post Oil's, during its two years it had a membership of ten community gardens in a catchment area that included Rockingham, Bellows, Saxtons River, Westminster, Cambridgeport, Grafton, and Athens. This project not only initiated three new community gardens during its first year, it also sponsored food and gardening workshops, and explored the possibility of developing a community high tunnel hoophouse. Additionally, the Collaborative partnered with the Bellows Falls Our Place food shelf, the Sustainable Valley Group, and the Greater Falls Connection regarding such concerns as continuing with the efforts to create a food hub in the area, and encouraging the availability of local food alternatives in area markets and school lunch programs.

These and other efforts have involved hundreds of people, most of whom were not staff of Post Oil, but without whom this emerging, community-based food system would not exist today. In recognition of this community effort, the Vermont Center for Sustainable Agriculture made Post Oil the recipient of its 2010 award, the first non-agricultural entity to receive this honor. This is a fitting tribute to all of us for our good beginning, and an inspiration for working on all that remains to be done.

CHAPTER 12

Who's at the Table?

BY ANGELA AND RICHARD BERKFIELD

I N building community the first logical step is to connect with people who are similar to us. People who have something in common can often build community quite easily. For many people in the Brattleboro area a community can be made up of friends who spend time doing activities together or supporting each other. In the case of Post Oil Solutions, our community initially was made up of people who were concerned about a post-oil world and wanted to act on this issue. This community has done some wonderful things together, and we celebrate that success.

As we look around at this Post Oil Solutions community, we see that most people are white, and most are middle- to upper-middle-class. As we have deepened our understanding of sustainable communities, we have learned that it isn't possible without social justice. For a community to be sustainable it is important that everyone, regardless of class, sex, or race, is working together to meet the needs of all. We see a need to break down a paternalistic "helping" mentality which however well-intentioned further compounds dependency, and start practicing solidarity, instead, which means that we are all in this together. In short, we need to recognize that "My wellbeing is tied up with your wellbeing."

It is a big challenge for most of us to connect with people who do not have the same background as we do. We must get out of our comfort zone and find common ground with others. Cross-class and cross-race relationships are not easy. There are centuries of distrust, stereotyping, and feelings of superiority and inferiority that we all need to overcome. But we need to continue building these relationships and the trust to work together.

In this spirit, Post Oil Solutions is being intentional about building community across class and race divides. While we have a lot to learn and practice to accomplish this, we do know that we don't want these socially created divisions to divide us anymore. In order to build true community, we need to learn about and understand the daily reality of people of color and the poor.

Some people say they see every human being as the same, despite color of skin or socioeconomic status, but the reality is that society does not consider all of us to be equal. White-skin privilege creates a different lived experience than for people of color. They and low-income folks in Brattleboro have told us how police, shopkeepers, and social service agencies treated them, and how it is a very different experience than respectful, polite, and courteous ways that we have had. While we are working toward the day that we are all treated equally, we have to be realistic about the racism and classism that is still prevalent today, both in interpersonal relationships and in the institutions of our society.

We feel that an attainable goal is for people to have well paying jobs; affordable, quality housing; affordable, quality health care; the ability to choose where they want to live and shop and go; and freedom from discrimination. To reach this goal, as a community, we need to learn how to work together. In addition, people at the decision-making table need to be representative of the community.

A question that often is asked is, "Why aren't more people of color and low income involved?" We are trying to ask in a different way, "What are we doing that is preventing people of color and low income from getting involved?" Post Oil Solutions is thinking about how to be a relevant organization to all people in the area. We aren't there yet, but we are working toward making a decision-making table with many voices.

Recently, Post Oil Solutions developed a Race and Class Committee that is holding the organization accountable to its values, mission, and goals. There are many things that we can do to move toward our goal. Our process has started with looking inward. We have done an Anti-Racist Assessment and a Class Assessment. We also have a discussion about race and class at our monthly meetings. This has allowed us to be more intentional and conscientious that we are inclusive of everyone in any project we initiate or become involved with.

This is all motivating us to be better listeners to what people in our community need so that we can develop projects to meet that need. Our main program area is building a community-based food system that was discussed earlier in the essay, "Building a Community-Based Food System." In doing so, we have seen how other issues, such as transportation and health care directly impact our food system. Unaffordable healthcare, for example, puts people in a tough spot financially, making it difficult for people to buy food and receive necessary treatment. "It's medicine or food," people have told us. Others have mentioned that when they don't feel well, they don't have the energy to garden or cook. Chronic and curable illnesses hinder our reaching our potential in building a community-based food system. For this reason, Post Oil Solutions is in support of the Healthcare Is a Human Right Campaign.

Each person has a story, and that story is related to the color of their skin and the amount of money in their pocket. But no matter what those stories are, they are all linked, and they all need to be told and heard if we are going to build the kind of community that meets the needs of all.

CHAPTER 13

The Neighborhood Market: Local Food for Local People

BY RICHARD BERKFIELD

S PRING marks the start of the growing season, with the promise of all of the delicious and nutritious food produced by our fertile soils. Unfortunately, many of us are not enjoying this bounty for a variety of reasons. As more and more people reconnect to their food and the soil and hands from which it comes, we need to make sure that all of our neighbors have the opportunity to do so as well. This vital connection has the potential to bring us together as strong communities to overcome many of the economic and environmental challenges that threaten the health and wellbeing of all of our neighbors.

Fortunately, for those of us without the space, time or green thumb for gardening, we have a lot of very talented, hard-working farmers whose very passion is to grow food for us to eat. There is a farmers market many days of the week: Wednesday in Brattleboro, Friday in Townshend and Bellows Falls, Saturday in Brattleboro, and Sunday in Putney. Often seen as the exclusive stomping ground of yuppies and hippies, farmers' markets are, plain and simple, a place to find fabulous food grown right in our community.

Let's face it: we all should be eating more vegetables, the fresher the better, but many of us simply can't afford the retail prices that farmers need to charge to make a living. As it currently exists, the food system just isn't set up in a way that supports farms, consumers, and communities. For the past five years, we at Post Oil Solutions have been asking what we can do about this. And as a result, we basically set out to do the impossible: to figure out how to better bridge the gap between farmers who need a reasonable price and consumers who need to get the most for their money.

How can this be done? We've asked around, and people have told us what they want. People want a market with a community focus, located close to home, that has reasonable prices, accepts EBT (formerly known as food stamps), involves residents from the neighborhood in the market's continued development, and gives helpful hints and recipes for cooking and storage. We envisioned this market as one where the community itself could be the middleman.

Hence, we created the Neighborhood Market. The Neighborhood Market is a market for people on a tight budget located in downtown Brattleboro. We have worked with the farmers to sell at a reduced price, and this arrangement satisfies them because we ask that market-goers commit to making weekly purchases the entire fifteen-week market season. A guaranteed market helps farmers run a more efficient business. A lower price is better for consumers. And the commitment is an opportunity for people to really dedicate themselves to eating fresh produce for the fifteen-week season. With farmers, market staff, and other participants eager to share their favorite tips and recipes, eating your veggies will become even easier to making a connection to local, nutritious food, farmers, and community.

This Neighborhood Market supports new farmers in their developing new markets, so we won't be taking opportunities away from existing farms. Our goal is to get more people to buy directly from their farmers and to get more community participation from individuals and organizations to support that change. From the beginning, we reached out to other organizations that were concerned about the health of their clients and staff to become partners in creating a fun and sustainable market. One of our new partners put it this way: "We are interested in working together to offer our clients better access to improved health and wellbeing." It is this collaborative spirit that is contributing to the market's success and making it fun! We are thankful to our volunteers and partners.

Finally, as the market continues to grow, we are raising funds so that we can make it the best market possible. It takes community support to build a community-based food system, one that provides food for all and a fair return on investment to farmers.

CHAPTER 14

Farmers' Markets: Affordable and Healthy Food

BY SHERRY MAHER

FARMERS markets are springing up all across the country. According to USDA statistics the growth in the number of farmers' markets between 1994 and 2010 was nearly 350 percent. And here in our corner of New England, we see that trend in action. Close to a dozen new farmers' markets have opened recently. Windham County alone saw a 40 percent growth in farmers' markets last year. Add to that the many markets operating through the winter and you can sense the explosion in farmers' markets around the country.

So what does all this have to do with building sustainable communities? With "local" being the current buzzword, farmers' markets can't be beat for keeping our dollars local—whether they're spent on parsley, pies or pottery. According to the Business Alliance for Local Living Economies (BALLE), a dollar spent at a local, independently owned business circulates longer here in our community than a dollar spent at a chain or box store, thus helping to strengthen the local economy.

But more importantly, giving more of our food dollars directly to our local farmers and bakers helps to keep them in the business of feeding us, providing safe, healthy food that wasn't trucked across the country, harvested before it was at its peak flavor or nutritional value, or loaded with chemicals and preservatives to keep it "fresh" for weeks in a package on a store shelf.

But not everyone sees a farmers' market as affordable, an inexpensive place to buy food. Many people are still under the false impression that fresh fruits and veggies are less expensive at nearby supermarkets.

But the facts show something different. Time after time, from Washington State, through Iowa and Ohio, all the way to Vermont, price comparison studies have found farmers' market prices for most fresh fruits and vegetables to be better than prices at grocery stores, especially for organic produce. Granted, there are also more expensive specialty items at a farmers' market, but the same holds true for the supermarket.

One of my favorite reports came from a frugal blogger looking for $5 dinners. She was surprised to find that farmers' markets had not only some of the best prices, but clearly the best quality and variety.

Furthermore, when a particular crop is at the height of its growing season, many farmers are quick to offer more of a break if you can buy in bulk.

But perhaps the most convincing report told of one farm whose owners compared its market prices against those of area supermarkets over the course of the growing season. They were even so bold as to take on a nearby Walmart, and they still found that many of their farmer's market prices throughout the growing season beat even the low-price giant.

But while this is all true, we also know that local food can be—and often is—more expensive than the offerings from your average supermarket or corner store. This is especially problematic for people living on marginal budgets, with food stamps that often are not sufficient to get a family through the month, much less maintain a healthy, nutritious diet of local food. That is why farmers' markets across the country, and especially here in Vermont, have made a special effort to provide EBT (electronic benefit transfer, aka "food stamps") access to local food for our more financially challenged neighbors. As anyone connected to an area food bank knows, this is a group of our neighbors who continues to grow because of high unemployment and, especially, the growing phenomenon of underemployment and low pay in the working class.

Both private and public funds support efforts to offset the expensive equipment costs of wireless card readers at farmers' markets, or of the wooden market tokens that are used in EBT transactions. Back in 1997, states were required to begin shifting their food stamp programs from the familiar coupons to an EBT process, which works like using a debit card. This new banking process for food stamps largely cut out our local farmers, farm stands, and farmers' markets. EBT-access projects, such as Brattleboro Area and Bellows Falls farmers' markets and Post Oil's Brattleboro Winter, have brought back to our local farmers many of the food-stamp dollars they previously accepting regularly from their EBT shoppers. At present, some 3,000 farmers' markets across the county accept EBT-purchases of food.

In addition to providing EBT access at farmers' markets, other incentive programs help cash-strapped families get fresher, healthy fruits and veggies for their food dollars. Here in Vermont, the Department of Children and Families distributes $30 coupon books to families enrolled in WIC (Women, Infants and Children), as well as to other income-eligible families and seniors. Another program offered for the last four years at many Vermont farmers' markets matched up to $10 in EBT purchases per market. A thrifty farmers' market shopper could budget $10 a week or $40 a month from their EBT benefits for farmers' market food shopping and by receiving the $10 market match turn that into $80, essentially doubling their money.

And some markets, like Post Oil's Brattleboro Winter Market, offer their Market Match program as another way of encouraging EBT shoppers to shop for local, farm-fresh food. We have seen a growing number of EBT-eligible customers who, after purchasing $10 worth of tokens each week, then received the maximum $10 Market Match coupon and expressed great relief and joy over how they are able to double their food purchasing power throughout the month. Supported by our coffee and tea sales at the Market, as well as raffles, donations, and small grants, Post Oil has been able to sustain this program thus far, though we're concerned about the growing food crisis in our world, and the increasing number of food-insecure people's potential to outstrip our efforts.

Additionally, there are new, specially formatted markets that are going even further to meet low-income community members more than half way. Post Oil has been one of the leaders of this movement, as seen with our Neighborhood Market, which has been on Elliot and Green Streets in more recent years, and at Westgate in West Brattleboro. (For a further description, see page XX, "The Neighborhood Market: Local Food for Local People").

Again, helping to make local food more affordable and accessible to all people in our communities is a win-win proposition for everyone. Not only are more people eating a nutritious, safe diet (with all the health implications you care to imagine), our area farmers are benefiting as well, along the local businesses that also receive those dollars.

CHAPTER 15

Toward a Community
of Gardeners

THERE are a number of qualities that a food system requires in order to be sustainable. Some of these we've written about in the preceding essays, like food justice, where a healthy, safe diet is accessible and affordable to all. Or a food system that is community-based, as opposed to being import-dependent, one that is focused on the business of feeding ourselves and our next-door and regional neighbors. This in turn, serves as the foundation of an agricultural economy and the ancillary jobs and enterprises it stimulates.

At the most basic level, a food system must keep us healthy and alive. In the context of the volatile, post-petroleum world we've entered, a sustainable food system must be increasingly local and decentralized, less dependent on fossil-fuel input, more redundant and resilient. It will be grounded not in considerations of the bottom line, but in taking care of our land, water, and air in perpetuity. It's this kind of vision that, when acted upon, allows for a sustainable diet right now and makes it possible for the future.

Finally, in the context of the growing evidence that climate change is developing exponentially, with dire consequences for our climate-dependent, fragile, industrial food system, feeding ourselves sustainably is particularly relevant. To do so, our concern and focus includes such matters as which food products will do best in our changing climate conditions, and can withstand the challenges of such things as excessive moisture, drought, and new pests.

There are at least three things we can be doing to grow a locally-based, regional food system. We should increasingly support our local and regional farmers; grow, preserve, and cook more food ourselves; and encourage our local, state and federal officials to both acknowledge food security for the serious issue that it is and adopt policies commensurate with this crisis. None of these are radical departures from the past and present practice of many Vermonters. Rather, what we're suggesting is that they now require a more concerted effort, one that results in a greater commitment to feeding ourselves.

We need to become a community of gardeners.

This is not to suggest that we will feed ourselves by our efforts alone. Despite some of the mythology that has developed around local food and the "hundred-mile diet" that people committed to limiting themselves when they undertook a week-long "Localvore Challenge," our ancestors, who basically fed themselves (because there were no supermarkets to run to!), also imported such items as salt, tea, coffee, and spices. Our local and regional farmers—even the industrial food system that is currently breaking down—are part of the food-security equation, and will remain so for the foreseeable future.

But in order to provide the resilience we will require to be food-secure, there is no substitute for our taking more responsibility for our own food, individually and collectively, as families and next door neighbors and members of neighborhood and community gardens, using containers, window boxes, nine-by-twelve lawns or empty lots, and through keeping bees, shared root cellars, hoophouses, and potluck socials. As people found by using their Victory Gardens during World War II, an incredible amount of food can be produced by an active, involved citizenry.

An example of this kind of effort is the Food Security Collaborative (formerly the Greater Falls Community Garden Collaborative). Emerging as a food security project at the end of 2011 from a series of community conversations about how to make locally produced food more accessible and affordable to everyone in the community, the Collaborative was a coalition of ten school and community gardens in Bellows Falls, plus Our Place Drop In Center, Sustainable Valley Group, Greater Falls Connects, and Post Oil Solutions, which initiated the project.

The vision of the Collaborative was to encourage everyone within the project's domain (Rockingham, Bellows Falls, Westminster, Saxtons River, Cambridgeport, Grafton, and Athens) to be involved in the production of their food. This is a most ambitious plan, and one that may take some time to realize, but as a grandmother of ten put it, "If you don't aim high, you might as well stay in bed."

To jump-start the project, people went to the voters at the Rockingham town meeting in March and the Bellows Falls village meetings in May 2012. In each instance, the Project was greeted with enthusiasm and $1,500 from each meeting to pursue these efforts. The good people of Rockingham repeated their act of generosity at their 2013 town meeting.

Collaborative members then began exploring a number of garden-site possibilities in our region, Over the two years of the project's existence, four gardens were started: the Atkinson Street Neighborhood Garden at the Meeting Waters YMCA and the Stone Church Community Garden, both in Bellows Falls; the Saxtons River Community School Garden at the Saxtons River Elementary School; and the Athens Community Garden which planted exclusively for the town food shelf that had recently started.

All of these efforts were exercises in neighborly collaboration. In the case of the Atkinson garden, twelve raised beds were put together, with a consensus that the people involved were going to share what they grew. In addition to the generosity of the taxpayers, financial support was found through grants from the New England Grassroots Environment Fund.

The Saxtons River project, which is located on the grounds of the Saxtons River Elementary School, began as the result of a community conversation organized by the Collaborative. From the beginning, it has been an endeavor that has involved community members, teachers, and students, as well as faculty and employees of Vermont Academy. Each of the five grades of students has a raised-bed garden, and is supported by the community in its work of creating and maintaining these beds.

The Athens garden was envisioned from the start by the six neighbors who came together on this project as an effort that would be devoted to raise fresh food for the town's people who used the new food shelf. Ninety pounds of potatoes and ninety-five pounds of carrots were realized in their first year.

The Collaborative was also able to provide valuable support to a number of ongoing school gardens through financial assistance and consultation.

The Collaborative also hosted an extensive workshop series during the non-growing season. The knowledge it imparted is essential for creating a community of gardeners. During the two years that it sponsored these events, the Collaborative presented a number of well attended sessions on canning, composting, soil preparation, garden planning, the nine-by-twelve garden, and inexpensive root-cellaring. They also offered several cooking workshops that demonstrated not only how to cook and incorporate local food items, but also how to do it economically and easily.

Unfortunately, the Food Security Collaborative has not been able to sustain itself. Its Coordinator left the project after two years, and a lack of funds prevented it from hiring a replacement.

However, most of the gardens continue into the 2015 growing season.

During its brief moment, the Collaborative did create a lot of interest in locally produced food. Many people became involved in learning about and growing, preserving, and cooking food from their gardens. Though the project has died, Post Oil Solutions will continue to support this community of gardeners who are now better able to provide for their own food security through the experience of feeding themselves by their own means.

PART III

Adaptation, Resistance... or Both?

YOU would think the news that, for the first time in human history, climate-warming greenhouse gas in our atmosphere has reached 400 parts per million would command much greater attention than being relegated to the Environment section of *The New York Times* and the back page of the weekend edition of the *Brattleboro Reformer*. While admittedly symbolic, and no worse than the 399 ppm of the day before, it's nevertheless a number that should give us pause. As *The Guardian UK* pointed out, "The last time so much greenhouse gas was in the air was several million years ago, when the Arctic was ice-free, savannah spread across the Sahara desert and sea level was up to 40 meters higher than today."

During the 12,000 years of human civilization, carbon dioxide levels in the atmosphere generally were stable at 280 ppm. But since the advent of the Industrial Revolution and the increased burning of fossil fuels, there has been a 42 percent increase. As a consequence, scientists fear that our species may be precipitating a return to "a prehistoric climate in which human societies will face huge and potentially catastrophic risks," according to Bob Ward, director at the Grantham Research Institute on Climate Change at the London School of Economics.

What makes this news especially unsettling is that it underscores that the level of carbon dioxide in the atmosphere is rising faster than it has in the past. When measurements of atmospheric CO2 first began in 1958, the level was 315 ppm. The average level is growing about 2 ppm per year, which is a hundred times faster than the rate of increase at the end of the last Ice Age. Obviously, despite the convincing scientific evidence and nearly unanimous consensus about climate change, its human catalyst, and the potential disaster this represents for the world, we've yet to commit seriously to the substantial reduction of carbon emissions that is required.

Professor Bob Watson, former chair of the Intergovernmental Panel on Climate Change (IPCC) and the British government's chief scientific adviser, commented, "Passing 400 ppm is indeed a landmark, and the rate of increase shows no sign of abating, due to a lack of political commitment." He went on to note that, despite the fact that the world's governments have agreed to keep the rise in global temperature (which has already risen by over 1° Centigrade) to 2°, the level beyond which catastrophic warming is thought to become unstoppable, "the world is now most likely committed to an increase in surface temperature of 3°C-5°C compared to pre-industrial times." As Ralph Keeling, who runs the monitoring program at the Scripps Institution of Oceanography, summarized, "It means we are quickly losing the possibility of keeping the climate below what people thought were possibly tolerable thresholds."

Are we beginning to feel our shoulder blades pressing up against the wall?

More to the point, will this grim milestone of 400 ppm serve as a wakeup call to focus us not only on how we're going to adapt to the world we've created, but also on how we can rapidly curtail the further burning of coal, gas, and oil, so that there's still a world within which to live? For this is the effort to which we need to commit ourselves in order to build sustainable, resilient, *livable* communities for ourselves. A successful transition to our new world will require both adaptation and resistance.

We have no choice but to adapt to a world that is already here. But we can choose when we will act seriously to pursue this task. Will we make a commitment now, in the early stages, when we're really not yet hurting that badly? Or later, when we will have been overwhelmed by our circumstances and will no longer have any choice?

Typically, we as a species don't respond with foresight or alacrity to situations requiring us to change. It's true that, at times, we have demonstrated our potential for coming together to work through crises selflessly and courageously. We'll need to draw upon this capacity in the years ahead if we are to survive.

But unfortunately, this will not be enough. As we've seen already, the effects of climate change are unpredictable, exponential, chaotic, and very destructive. The period of long emergencies we may face will require a level of social welfare that is beyond the stamina of individual spontaneity or institutional goodwill to provide solely. We need to be coming together now, as families, neighborhoods, communities, towns, and regions, to make adaptation to a changing world both a priority and a regular habit of our personal and public lives. We need to learn to make the business of taking care of each other and ourselves around such essentials as food, transportation, health care, home heating, and emergency preparedness a part of our daily routine, especially in those ways that we presently depend upon the transnational corporation or federal government to do for us.

For a post-oil age, sustainable and resilient communities are also intentional groups, ones that are fashioned on the basis of the kind of commitment that will be required of us to deal with the changes and disruptions in our lives we can reasonably anticipate from climate change, and not the episodic, spontaneous, gatherings they are now, brought about by an emergency. They are created conscientiously, before a crisis occurs, with the understanding that while we're entering uncharted waters, we nevertheless can do things now, in those necessary areas mentioned above on the basis of what we do know. However tentative, imperfect, and always subject to change such a process is, intentional efforts are the best preparation to meet what comes next in our lives. It makes climate change a part of our everyday consciousness and lives, hence less likely that we will be at square one, completely unprepared as the crisis becomes more immediate and drastic. By collaborating now, we can build the community infrastructure— the social glue—that will allow us to meet the basic needs of each other and ourselves in a post-petroleum world.

But we must do more. Adapt, for sure, become increasingly self- and community-sufficient, but we also need to resist the extraction and burning of fossil fuels.

For it has become increasingly clear that it is not enough to build resilient, collaborative, socially just communities if, at the same time, we're not addressing Big Oil, the corporate state, and the energy policy they pursue that threatens to drive humanity over the climate-cliff. On the same day that scientists announced that the Earth was now warming fifty times faster than it ever had and that carbon dioxide levels had set a new record, Exxon's $100,000-a-day CEO, Rex Tillerson, bragged that he expected renewables would account for just one percent of our energy in 2040, and said, "My philosophy is to make money." To have any reasonable chance of living in sustainable communities, we need to resist this kind of attitude that is responsible for the fix that we're in. Likewise, we have to resist the politics of fossil fuel that serves as the basis of President Obama's "all of the above" energy policy, where oil and gas are as welcome as solar and wind. To have any future worth living for our children and grandchildren, we need to create a political climate that will convince Big Oil to walk away from trillions of dollars of profits in Alberta's tar sands, North Dakota's Bakken shale formation, and the Arctic's waters.

We must accept the fact that what is needed is the "massive intervention" that Bill McKibben calls for, one that he describes as already developing. From blocking the Keystone XL pipeline and fracking wells around the country and closing dozens of new coal plants to fighting for fossil-fuel divestment at university and college campuses, non-profit foundations, city municipalities and religious denominations, there's a growing movement of citizens who are saying, "No, we can't afford to burn the stuff."

Just as we all need to be part of the effort to create resilient communities, so too do we need to be active in this grassroots resistance to Big Oil and its threat to our existence. That is the only way we can stop the madness that presently dominates our body politic.

CHAPTER 16

Post Politics

POLITICS is the bane of our existence. From the halls of government and the corporate suites, to our schools, workplaces, communities, and homes, politics—the use of power to dominate and control others, to exert power-over—is the basis of the pain and suffering that all too often characterize human relationships. Quite simply, politics is responsible for much of what's wrong in the world, the reason why many of us are angry and unhappy with the way life is.

Politics is an inherently adversarial relationship, us vs. them, one-up over one-down. And while force and violence may not always express themselves overtly, their threat is omnipresent, even when they come dressed in the smile of "reasonableness."

The need to be in control is rooted in ego, that part of human nature that invariably gets us into trouble when we allow it to dictate our behaviors in the world.

This understanding is important when envisioning what a resilient, sustainable community might look like in a post-petroleum world. To realize this goal, it's not sufficient to only consider the things we need to do—e.g., grow our own food, build a local economy, develop renewable sources of energy, create an alternative to fossil-fuel transportation, move beyond our consumer-based culture, and so on. As important as these are, there is the equally critical question of how we go about accomplishing these tasks. If a community is to be truly sustainable, it must avoid going about doing business as usual, in the ways that have gotten us into the unsustainable fix we're presently in. From our most public and impersonal to our most intimate and personal interactions, we have to bring what we do in line with the values of the sustainable world we're trying to create. A sustainable community can only be realized through a transformative practice that allows for a sustainable community.

Therefore power, and its exercise in the world, needs to be reconsidered. Not only must we understand that, ultimately, the effort to dominate and control life is a fool's errand, an impossible mission that can only lead to eventual disaster, as climate change makes so abundantly clear, but that it's also counterproductive to the quality existence we all want and are capable of realizing. To live life the way we need to in order to be sustainable partners with the rest of life requires an approach that allows for and accommodates the existence of the other. We need to accept life as it is, and to allow it to exist. In so doing, we need to forgo a self-serving view of the way we believe life should be, which invariably results in pain and suffering, death and destruction. Rather, our conduct must be informed with a modesty and humility sufficient to assuming our true proportions as a living being sharing life on this planet with other living beings, honoring our interdependent position within the larger scheme of things, and taking up no more space than what we reasonably require.

Behaving in sync with the values of a sustainable existence, however, is a slippery slope. Living in the political world as we do, this can easily fall prey to "political correctness." Rather than serving as a gentle guide, behaviors can become codified, instead, made into instruments that are used to define people as "acceptable," or not, and reward or punish them, accordingly. Judgment supplants acceptance, politicizing the interaction—us over them—thus personalizing what is otherwise a neutral encounter. Rather than accepting people and ourselves for the imperfect beings that we are, and learning to live with each other as best we can, it reduces interactions to exercises in domination and control: "correct" behavior over that which is deemed "incorrect." This is fatal to a sustainable existence, for it threatens the interpersonal integrity of generosity, compassion, and lovingkindness that is essential to a viable, seven generation community.

But as we live in the political world, one that is suffused with power-relationships, how do we avoid this trap and make a successful transition from our present power arrangements to the more accepting ones that most of us would prefer?

This has long been the dilemma of humankind. We want the life we don't live, yet live the life we don't want. Resolving this ancient contradiction is essential if we are to survive the unsustainable cul-de-sac that this contradiction has led us into.

What is to be done?

The short answer—and, in reality, the only practical response—is that we just do it. We act in prefigurative ways as if the society of humans we seek actually exists. In much the way that Gandhi said that we must be the change we want to see in the world, so do we need to act, now, as the people who, to the best of our individual and collective abilities, live by the vision of what it means to be a sustainable people. With all our imperfections, we leap into the void of walking the talk. This is all we can do. But fortunately it's good enough, because it's precisely what needs to be done.

It's important to emphasize, however, that we do this within the context of the political world we live in. We need to avoid another danger of the aforementioned slippery slope, of trying to realize a sustainable community by removing ourselves from a world we judge corrupt and irredeemable, and living, instead, in some kind of utopian ghetto with other true believers. Rather, it's important that we engage with our world, and to do so by accepting it as it is.

In this manner, we steer clear of power struggles, and the destructive adversarial energy they generate. We discover common ground with others, instead, upon which we can move forward. The outcome may not always be what either of us originally envisioned; but the very act of choosing to involve ourselves with others from a post-political perspective will be a significant contribution toward creating the sustainable community we desire.

CHAPTER 17

Food Democracy: GMO-Labeling and the Food Sovereignty Movement

HERE is much that goes into building a community-based food system (see Chapter 10, for example), one that allows us to be food-sufficient people who are secure in both the quantity and quality of our food supply. It must have a strong agricultural base, made up of small and medium-sized farmers who produce a sustainable, affordable, healthy diet for everyone. It must also be populated by a citizenry that takes responsibility for its food by supporting local farmers and by undertaking individual and collective efforts at gardening, canning, root-cellaring, seed-saving, and the like. In short, a community-based food system is one in which we, the people, take charge of what we feed ourselves and our loved ones.

But there are economic and political forces that oppose such expressions of community power and independence. Building food hubs and organizing farm-to-school programs, sponsoring workshops and running farmers' markets, alone, is not sufficient. We also have to deal with the profit-driven, government-subsidized, and petroleum-dependent industrial food system that threatens the development of such an autonomous, localized system.

Increasingly, the effort to build sustainable communities includes political struggles. Not only do we need to become more collaborative, resilient, socially just, and self-sufficient to achieve our purpose, we also have to be prepared to meet political challenges. Given the inherent conflict between the values and behaviors of these two approaches—conflict and competition vs. cooperation and generosity, the end justifies the means vs. the importance of the process, deception and betrayal vs. honesty and integrity—creative tension results.

As we've argued previously, politics is not the path to building truly sustainable communities. To make a community sustainable requires its citizens to eliminate the "us-versus-them," zero-sum dynamic that is the essence of politics, as well as of the power-relationships that inevitably enforce such divisions. A viable post-petroleum community, with its need for people to be working together to promote the survival and well-being of all, can't afford the luxury of a politicized social environment that divides us from one another. The need to collaborate and cooperate is too important to engage in such a destructive self-indulgence.

Yet, we also live in the political world. As our skeptics continually (but correctly) remind us, we have to be practical and realistic. We can't simply walk away from the political reality that is so much a part of human experience, creating some sanitized utopian enclave, immune from this basic fact of life. Politics is us, whether we like it or not.

The issue, therefore, is not to deny or avoid, but rather to swim skillfully and wholesomely in the muck of political existence. That is, we need to act effectively with those social forces that seek to dominate and exploit, while remaining true to the values of a sustainable community.

How do we address the political challenges to sustainable communities that are increasingly presenting themselves by the corporate state?

Two issues that reflect this concern are the genetically engineered (GE) crops that are already in sixty to seventy percent of processed food, and the Food Safety and Modernization Act, enacted in 2011, that could ruin many small farmers through regulations whose costs, while within the means of industrial farmers, could be prohibitive to smaller farmers, putting some of them out of business, as a consequence.

⌒

At present, there aren't any regulatory requirements for the long-term testing of genetically engineered food for potential risks to human health. Unlike new drugs, which require strict safety evaluations for approval, there are no mandatory human clinical trials for GE crops. This is despite the fact that scientists have found that the insecticide in GE corn is showing up in our bloodstream and in the umbilical-cord blood of pregnant women.

Given the absence of conclusive information about genetically-engineered food, and the growing suspicions about its potential harm (several National Academy of Sciences studies, for example, have affirmed that GE crops have the potential to introduce new toxins, carcinogens, and allergens into our food), Just Label It has built its campaign on the common sense principle that until we know that GE crops are safe, people should at least be informed about their presence in their food so that they make a choice about whether or not they want to eat them.

This is the opinion of ninety-three percent of the polled American public that believes people have the right to be informed about the presence of genetically altered ingredients in their food. Sixty-four countries, including the fifteen member states of the European Union, Japan, Australia, Brazil, Russia, and China have laws requiring the labeling of genetically engineered foods. The national Just Label It campaign has submitted over a million signatures to the FDA asking the agency to require the labeling of GE foods. In short, there appears to be wide support for the notion that people have a right to know what's in their food.

Not surprisingly, there is a lot public support for such action in Vermont and our region of the state, in particular. At present, a GMO-labeling bill was passed in the Vermont Legislature during the 2014 legislative session, and was signed by Governor Peter Shumlin, reversing a position he had taken the previous year. Additionally, the states of Maine and Connecticut have passed similar legislation, but unlike Vermont's bill, their implementation is contingent upon five other northeastern states' following suit.

Labeling efforts, however, have met with stiff opposition, as evidenced by the $70 million that corporate opponents of such laws poured into campaigns of fear and misinformation to defeat California's Proposition 37 in November, 2012 as well as Washington state's L-522 a year later, both of which would have required labeling. More recently, similar efforts have been responsible for defeating labeling propositions in Oregon and Colorado. And of course, Vermont's law is being challenged in court by Monsanto.

There's no wonder, of course, that Monsanto and their biotech allies fight such efforts. Informed consumers do not want to purchase or consume GE foods because of the possibility that they present health risks.

As a Monsanto executive acknowledged years ago, "If you put a label on genetically engineered food you might as well put a skull and crossbones on it."

But while there is progress by states to enact GMO-labeling laws (over twenty have introduced such legislation), there is also an effort by Monsanto, the Grocery Manufacturers Association, and their biotech and industrial food allies to undermine this progress by pushing the U.S. Food and Drug Administration (FDA) to finalize its 2001 guidelines on voluntary labeling of

GMOs. On the surface, this would seem to be a move that would benefit consumers. However, this is not the mandatory labeling consumers are fighting for; a federal voluntary labeling plan plays right into the hands of the industry.

For one thing, the FDA's guidance on voluntary GMO-labeling could be used to put an end to existing, legitimate, voluntary non-GMO-labeling efforts that have been taking place in such places as our own Brattleboro and Putney Food Co-ops. By referring to their previous ruling that GMO and non-GMO foods are "substantially equivalent," the FDA could rule against non-GMO or GMO-free labels on the basis that they mislead consumers by implying that there's a difference between GMO and non-GMO foods.

Worse yet, the FDA could also take away states' rights to pass GMO-labeling laws on the basis of its highly controversial ruling that GMO and non-GMO foods are "substantially equivalent." Once the FDA finalizes its GMO-labeling guidelines, the industry can then use this to preempt state laws requiring the mandatory labeling of GMOs. States currently have the right to enact GMO-labeling laws precisely because the FDA has not formally ruled on GMO-labeling.

The current law supports states' rights to enact their own food-labeling laws, as long as two conditions are met. First, the state must produce compelling evidence that the law is needed to protect the health or safety of citizens. And secondly, there must be no pre existing FDA regulation governing the label in question. The GMO-labeling laws being considered and enacted by various states meet those conditions. But that could change if the FDA finalizes its 2001 guidelines on voluntary GMO-labeling. This is why Monsanto and the Grocery Manufacturers Association, which spend millions of dollars to defeat GMO-labeling legislation whenever they've appeared, have also publicly endorsed the FDA's 2001 guidelines.

In short, this potential FDA ruling to prohibit voluntary GMO-labeling could wipe out the efforts of citizens to enact mandatory labeling laws through state legislatures and federal regulatory agencies, which at least ninety-three percent of the public agrees is a perfectly reasonable requirement. There is a serious disconnect here between the voice of the people and our government in Washington. The biotech industry and its industrial-food allies, like the fossil-fuel, pharmaceutical, and other transnational industries, exert inordinate power over our nation's political processes. With the money they lavish on our elected officials, they are able to dictate policies, rules, and regulations that benefit them and their pursuit of profit while being at the expense of the rest of us.

It is in this context of a compromised democracy that we can begin to consider and act upon our alternatives. We might be better advised, for example, rather than trying to make an unresponsive government accede to our reasonable demands, to put our time and energy instead into initiating local and regional actions that might advance our cause more immediately and effectively. We need to empower ourselves by taking greater responsibility for realizing our goals through actions of our own, and not solely by depending upon the corporate state to do the job for us.

We can begin with such a simple step as educating ourselves and others about what we can do to avoid GE foods, until there is sufficient evidence that they are not harmful. Knowing that the best option is to buy USDA-certified organic products, and that these standards prohibit the use of GMOs, is a first step. Arming ourselves and others with the kind of information found in the Center for Food Safety's "True Food Shopper's Guide: How to Avoid Foods Made with GMOs," while helping to raise awareness that sixty to seventy percent of processed foods available in grocery stores contain some GE material can help us to take more control of the food we eat.

We can make a point, as well, of increasingly buying our food from local farmers, through CSAs (Community Supported Agriculture), farm stands, and local stores that carry their products. These are people whom we can trust because their livelihood is dependent upon maintaining their reputation in their communities for providing healthy, nutritious, safe food.

Efforts to convince our grocery stores that it's good business to carry more organic, non-GMO products should be successful given the state where we live, but if they are not, we can do what others have done before: organize community buying clubs where you can get the organic, non-GMO food that you want.

Even more empowering, however, is the growing and raising of our own food. We can garden, can and store food, extend the season, save our seeds, even cook our own food—or we can learn to do so. Though fundamental to life, itself, food is not rocket science.

We can also do this with neighbors. Communities of gardeners who come together around their basic need to provide for their diet experience a very rewarding sense of self and community sufficiency.

What all of these suggestions illustrate is that we can move beyond simply insisting upon our right to know what's in our food to empowering ourselves, instead, by acting on this right through direct action. We can assume greater responsibility for our food, and, thus, begin to increasingly be less dependent upon playing the political game with its loaded dice.

⸜

Food sovereignty is the logical evolution of the local food movement. It's the next step to becoming an empowered citizenry, taking responsibility for what we eat. As a movement, it came to prominence recently when the federal Food Safety and Modernization Act was introduced in Congress. Enacted in response to the understandable alarm over the estimated 3,000 Americans who die each year from food-borne illnesses, the bill has desirable health and safety features that would better protect consumers from tainted food.

The problem is that the stricter oversight and regulations will not only apply to industrial agriculture—which is largely responsible for the outbreaks of contaminated food—but to small farmers as well, who sell directly to local customers. This will entail expenses that, while easily assumed by large agribusinesses, threaten to put many small farmers out of business. Forums and meetings that have been held in our region about this issue confirm that local farmers are very concerned.

Alarmed by this possibility, states such as Wyoming, Georgia, and North Carolina have introduced protective legislation. Towns in Massachusetts, Vermont, California, and Maine have passed home rule ordinances that assert the right of citizens to produce, process, sell, purchase, and consume local foods, without federal and state regulations to impede or usurp a citizen's right to foods of their choice. Their goal is to maintain control of food at the local level by asserting the right to remain autonomous from onerous government regulations, and the corporate industrial food system that it serves.

The ten towns in Maine—Penobscot, Sedgwich, Blue Hill, Trenton, Hope, Plymouth, Livermore, Appleton, Brooksville and Isle au Haut—passed ordinances between 2011 and 2013 that read like a localvore's Declaration of Independence. These Local Food and Self-Governance Ordinances assert that towns can determine their own food and farming policies locally, and exempt direct food sales between farmers and consumers from state and federal requirements. Producers and processors are protected from licensure in sales between them and a patron that are conducted for home consumption at farmers' markets, or at a roadside stand. The ordinances specifically note the right of the people to food sovereignty.

Not surprisingly, this has placed towns on a collision course with their state's Agriculture Departments, the latter often serving as an agent of the USDA. At the heart of these efforts is the inherent conflict that sustainable communities present to the corporate state in their efforts to be self-sufficient and, hence, independent. As one of these ordinances reads, *"our right to a local food system requires us to assert our inherent right to self-gov-*

ernment." This includes sales of raw milk and locally slaughtered meats. The food sovereignty ordinance that was passed by the citizens of Sedgwick, Maine, reads in part: *"Patrons purchasing food for home consumption may enter into private agreements with those producers or processors of local foods to waive any liability for the consumption of that food. Producers or processors of local foods shall be exempt from licensure and inspection requirements for that food as long as those agreements are in effect."*

If the courts rule against the local communities in their attempts to assert their food sovereignty rights, and the state attempts to close down farmers, resistance could move from working within the system to nonviolent direct action, with communities rallying to defend those so threatened, while at the same time creating guerrilla methods of producing and distributing local food.

Not surprisingly, the Maine Department of Agriculture has challenged these ordinances, threatening to fine and close down farms that ignore USDA rules. A Superior Court, for example, ruled against Dan Brown, a Blue Hill farmer who has been selling unlabeled, unlicensed raw milk.

This is to be expected, of course. After all, food sovereignty is a movement for radical change in the food system. Because it is about the democratic control of the food system, and the right of all people to define their own agrifood systems through a rescaling of food production away from the present industrial-scale production to local and regional scales, it is a threat to the interests of corporate agribusiness.

Essentially, food sovereignty is about the right of people to choose how we feed ourselves. It is reclaiming our right as communities to control our food system from seed to table and to produce, process, sell, and consume our local foods as we decide. In so doing, it also helps to preserve family farms and the tradition of selling food to our neighbors. As such, our right to a local food system is founded upon our inherent right to self-government.

Where this movement might go was suggested in a remark of G.W. Martin, a sixth-generation farmer from Montville, Maine, at a public hearing in 2013 concerning the selling of unlicensed raw milk: "If we have to go underground with food, we don't care."

This is the potential trajectory of the local food movement that began with localvore eat local challenges and the growing preference of citizens for the healthier, more nutritious and safer offerings of their local farmers to the challenge to this movement by industrial agriculture and its ally, the corporate state. People deciding—and acting upon—what is best for them is what democracy is all about.

CHAPTER 18

Election 2012:
The Politics
of Climate Silence

How relevant for us was the 2012 election to decide who would lead our country over the following four years? How relevant will it be in 2016?

How germane could it be when the issue of our time—global warming and climate change—was hardly mentioned by either the Republican or Democratic candidates, much less addressed as an urgent priority of the next administration?

If we are to survive as a species, we've got to get serious about reducing carbon emissions. We need to turn off the spigot of greenhouse-gas emissions as much and as quickly as we can. We must reduce greatly the burning of fossil fuels. There is no other choice. We're running out of time.

Needless to say, this is a challenging task, given our dependency upon petroleum for so much of what we take for granted to sustain us. But we can learn to live a less petroleum-intensive existence. We have the technical knowledge and the wherewithal. A sustainable way of life is not beyond our individual and collective abilities.

Rather, the problem is that the decision to burn less oil is not up to us, alone, despite the fact that we live in a society that is greatly dependent on fossil fuels for almost anything we can name. But it's also a political decision, one that is directed by the CEOs and investors of the oil corporations, who up to this point have clearly demonstrated that their priority is to drill, baby, drill. In following this path, they have the full support of both major parties in Congress and whoever is in the White House, all of whom receive millions of dollars in campaign contributions from Big Oil.

A meaningful reduction in the burning of carbon requires a degree of political courage that is absent at present. It would require our elected leaders not only to acknowledge the 900-pound climate elephant that is sitting on all of our laps, but more importantly, to disempower the oil industry from exercising such an unfair influence over our nation's energy policy.

How realistic was it to expect such courage from one presidential candidate, who denied the existence of global warming and climate change, or from the other, who supports tar sands and offshore drilling?

Future generations will be stunned by the politics of climate silence that characterized the 2012 Campaign. They probably will remark that this was a missed opportunity to rally public support (polls show, for example, that two-thirds of Americans would back an international agreement to cut carbon emissions globally by ninety percent by 2050) and make this issue the priority it should be. They will shake their heads in disbelief as to how we remained inactive in the face of the observable fact that, rather than being "hundred year events," the new normal is increasingly and more consistently characterized by "exceptional" weather.

What are we to do, then, when droughts and heat waves and the dire consequences they have for our industrial food system don't receive the attention and concern one should expect from Presidential aspirants?

What are we to do when this reflects a larger political arrangement in which the 1% exercises inordinate power over the rest of us?

There are several options to consider. The first, of course, is to exercise once again the "vote-for-the-lesser-of-two-evils" approach, in the hope that it'll work this time. Obama at least admits that "climate change is not a hoax," so one could fantasize that, if re-elected, he might become the President he promised to be when he ran for office in 2008.

Or one could join with the wonderfully sane Bill McKibben in his more promising effort to build "a campaign to directly confront the economic power of the fossil fuel industry" with the message that "it's not OK to sacrifice our future for the sake of one industry's bottom line." Following his watershed article in the August 2, 2012 issue of *Rolling Stone*, he has argued that over the past few months our planet has provided stark warning signs that humans have never seen before. Because of these, McKibben has been calling for direct action against the oil giants, including a divestment strategy of the kind that was successful in helping end apartheid in South Africa in the 1980s. "This is, at bottom, a moral issue," he wrote "we have met the enemy and they is [*sic*] Shell."

But as necessary as it is to stop oppressive power, we need to do this in a manner that is harmonious with our egalitarian, democratic, pacific values, and in a way that does not reproduce the power dynamic of "us versus them." The antidote for a political problem is ultimately non-political. Political solutions invariably beget political problems because they are about the distribution and exercise of political power, which is always at the heart of the conflict to begin with. Continuing with this adversarial approach guarantees that, rather than evolving solutions in which the needs and interests of all parties are considered, we end up once again with a process whereby one side imposes its political will on the other. Hence, rather than finally being broken, the cycle of one-up over one-down continues yet one more time.

How do we change this dynamic? How do we develop relationships that transcend power arrangements and political agendas while at the same time dealing effectively with the unavoidable conflicts that arise in life?

This process begins with the face-to-face relationships in our homes, schools, workplaces, and communities. This is where our social reality is created, which then plays out on the larger stage of national headlines and world events.

Relationships beyond politics are ultimately rooted in our acceptance of each other for the people we are. When this essential valuing of life is operative, relationships are characterized by common acts of kindness and compassion, modesty and selflessness, honesty and courage, fairness and respect. These behaviors, in turn, weave a web out of every day, interpersonal moments that provide the social integrity—the existential power—to be responsible for the wellbeing of ourselves and our neighbors and to deal effectively with our adversaries. It is the power of being a living instance of the world we all seek.

CHAPTER 19

Resistance

W HILE engaging in political struggles is counterproductive to creating sustainable communities, it also has become increasingly clear that communities of this kind are not enough by themselves. Building resilient, collaborative, socially just communities will not be sufficient if, at the same time, we're not also addressing Big Oil, the corporate state, and their energy policy, which threatens to drive humanity over the climate cliff of no return. To have any reasonable chance of living in sustainable communities, we need to stop this recklessness. We have to resist the politics of fossil fuel.

With the increase in the price of oil over the years after 2008 as the existing fields of inexpensive "sweet crude" peaked at approximately eighty-five million barrels per day (mbd), petroleum companies were awash in the cash they needed to engage in previously prohibitive exploration and drilling. They subsequently engaged in hydraulic fracturing thousands of feet under the ground, heated tar sands, and drilled miles beneath the ocean's surface in their efforts to tap unconventional sources. In so doing, they and their allies have jubilantly proclaimed the end of peak oil. Boasted Charles Drevna of the American Fuel and Petrochemical Manufacturers, "We're talking decades, if not into the hundreds of years, of supply in North America."

But as the melting Arctic, the frequency of catastrophic hundred-year weather events, serial heat waves and droughts, and the accelerated vanishing of many animal and plant species so graphically demonstrate, this is suicidal. The Earth is now warming fifty times faster than it ever has, and atmospheric carbon dioxide levels have set a new record.

As I have mentioned previously, Bill McKibben has brought to our attention three critical numbers that we need to keep in mind. First, if we're to avoid catastrophic consequences, we must keep the increase in global temperature below two degrees Celsius. As it is, the 1°C it has already risen has caused far more damage, from killer storms and droughts, to ocean acidification and species extinction, than had been predicted. Secondly, scientists estimate that humans can put about 565 more gigatons of carbon dioxide into the atmosphere and still hope to stay below 2°C. But third, the amount of fossil fuel that is in the ground and that we're planning to burn would release at least 2,795 gigatons. "We have five times as much oil and coal and gas on the books as climate scientists think is safe to burn," McKibben concluded. "We'd have to keep eighty percent of those reserves locked away underground to avoid that fate. Before we knew those numbers, our fate had been likely. Now, barring some massive intervention, it seems certain."

The Obama Administration's rhetoric notwithstanding, it's unrealistic to expect an intervention of this kind from the White House. His "all of the above" energy policy, where oil and gas are as welcome as solar and wind, clearly reveals a President who is either dangerously out of touch with reality, or who chooses to ignore this reality in favor of the trillions of dollars' worth of oil in Canada's tar sands and North Dakota shale from which Big Oil refuses to walk away. Despite what he said in his campaign speeches, which suggested that he's aware of climate change and the danger that it represents to humanity, his actions are quite different. Nowhere was this more plainly revealed than in a speech he gave in Cushing, Oklahoma, in 2012:

"Over the last three years, I've directed my administration to open up millions of acres for gas and oil exploration across twenty-three different states. We're opening up more than seventy-five percent of our potential oil resources offshore. We've quadrupled the number of operating rigs to a record high. We've added enough new oil and gas pipeline to encircle the Earth, and then some... In fact, the problem... is that we're actually producing so much oil and gas... that we don't have enough pipeline capacity to transport all of it where it needs to go."

No, we should not look to our President to be the "massive intervention" we need. We the people will have to be that, instead, and join the movement which has been building in recent years. From blockage of infrastructure and other acts of non-violent direct action, to the growing divestment campaign on college campuses, and the historical Peoples Climate March in New York City in September, 2014, there's a growing movement of citizens who are resisting the burning of fossil fuels. We all need to be part of this resistance. Driving a Prius, hanging our laundry on a clothesline, and joining a community garden are all great things, but they're not enough if we don't stop Big Oil in its mad pursuit of its bottom line. Activists who are fighting the good fight with other causes must now come together around an Occupy Climate Change, the ultimate cause, the one that not only embodies everything we're all struggling for, but also that which, if we don't win, will render moot all other political issues.

Much as it is when our lives are endangered by a thief invading our home or a predator stalking our neighborhood, we need to become a community of resistance to Big Oil's threat to our existence. Within the values of the sustainable communities we're trying to create at the same time, our resistance involves disarming, restraining, and pacifying, not injuring or killing. Just as we oppose and defend against the efforts of those who endanger our lives, we do so by refraining from similar behavior. We just want to live and let live.

CHAPTER 20

Fracking and Vermonters

Is fracking an issue for Vermonters?

It would appear that this question was answered decisively when Vermont became the first state in the union to ban fracking, along with the importation and storage of the toxic wastewater associated with that process.

When Governor Shumlin signed H.464 on May 17, 2012, he did so with the awareness that fracking has contaminated groundwater in states like Texas, Wyoming, and Pennsylvania and that Congress has exempted hydraulic fracturing from regulation under the Clean Water and Safe Drinking Water Acts. The Governor noted that "Very soon there is going to be a shortage of clean water on this planet. Drinking water will be more valuable than oil or natural gas. Human beings have survived for thousands of years without oil or natural gas. We have never known humanity or life on this planet to survive without clean water."

Shumlin again demonstrated his grasp of the climate crisis this past February when, in support of Senator Bernie Sanders' co-sponsorship of the Senate's Climate Protection Bill, he stated, "We cannot act quickly enough to move our nation and our planet off fossil fuels, reduce carbon emissions, and promote safe, renewable sources of energy."

This is all well and good. But as President Obama, for one, has demonstrated on all too many occasions, fine sounding words from politicians' mouths don't necessarily translate into commensurate deeds, especially when they bump up against the profit-seeking needs of the corporate world. And while the fracking ban is positive, it's largely symbolic because Vermont has little to no natural gas or oil. The real test of where we, as a state, stand on this issue arrived when our elected and appointed officials were confronted by a fossil-fuel corporation seeks to pursue a project in Vermont that is contrary to the values and sentiments expressed by our governor. To date, the same Governor who signed the bill banning fracking in Vermont has supported a project that would bring fracked gas into Vermont.

Vermont Gas Systems (VGS) has proposed the largest expansion of fossil-fuel infrastructure in Vermont in nearly fifty years. Until 2015, it was in the planning and permitting stages of a major natural gas transmission pipeline expansion in Addison County that would extend from Colchester to Vergennes and Middlebury, then under Lake Champlain to Ticonderoga, New York, to serve the International Paper Company. They have since decided to not go forward with the Phase 2 of their project, but continue to pursue plans to build a pipeline to Rutland and to connect to the US transmission lines in New York.

VGS is owned by GazMetro, the Canadian corporation that also owns Green Mountain Power, which in turn, through its recent purchase of Central Vermont Public Service (CVPS,) now controls over seventy percent of Vermont's electricity. Furthermore, GazMetro is owned in large part by Enbridge, the world's largest distributor of tar-sands oil and the same company that spilled one million gallons of tar-sands oil into the Kalamazoo River in July 2010. Enbridge is currently attempting to build a tar-sands pipeline from Alberta to Montreal, where it would connect to Portland Montreal Pipeline, which crosses Vermont's Northeast Kingdom.

VGS has admitted that gas transported through the pipeline will be derived in part from fracking in Canada. Not only does hydraulic fracturing contaminate drinking water, it also consumes between 2 and 8 million gallons of water per well. And contrary to the claims of its apologists that fracked gas is a bridge to green energy, it really acts more like a gangplank because the natural gas that is harvested, as well as that which leaks from wells, pipelines, and the fracking process is mostly methane, a greenhouse gas twenty-one times more impactful than carbon dioxide according to the EPA.

The decision as to whether to go forward has been halted by the Vermont Public Service Board's withdrawal of the original Certificate of Public Good that it granted VGS because of the substantial increase in expense that would be passed on to the ratepayers. Not surprisingly, however, the original approval process was highly flawed, with groups opposed to the expansion being denied intervener status by the PSB in part because "such status will unduly delay the proceeding or prejudice the interests of existing parties or of the public." This concern, however, didn't prevent large corporations, such as International Paper and IBM, from being allowed to participate.

Residents of Addison County, who are most directly impacted, are organizing to stop this project from being built on their land. Many residents of the towns along the route of the proposed pipeline have been organizing to voice their concerns about the project at their towns' select boards, particularly around the issue of the pipeline going through their properties.

Opposition to the project, in part, centers on the fact that the proposed route has Vermonters' homes situated permanently within the "Potential Impact Radius," the area within which everything could be destroyed in the event of an accident. Additionally, while Vermont has banned hydraulic fracturing within its borders, the VGS project would increase the utilization of fracked gas within the state. If Vermonters believe that fracking is so dangerous to humans and deleterious to the environment, why is it OK for Vermont to import fracked gas from Canada?

And why would we want GazMetro and Enbridge, a Canadian company, to extend its power over the environment and the economy of our state?

The proposed pipeline is a false solution to the climate crisis. Any investment in fossil-fuel infrastructure locks us into decades of fossil-fuel consumption, in order for investors to make a return.

We can express our solidarity with our northern neighbors by joining with them in their demonstrations or the PSB hearings, and showing that this issue involves all Vermonters who are concerned about climate change.

CHAPTER 21

Climate Justice or
"Climate Fascism"?

As part of his quest to burnish his tarnished legacy after six disappointing years in office, President Obama recently announced that the United States will contribute $3 billion over the next four years to the United Nations Green Climate Fund, a project to direct funds from wealthy countries to developing ones to help them slash emissions and adapt to global warming.

While it's not clear where the funding will come from, or whether Obama will need congressional approval (a certain defeat, if he does), the money is nevertheless contingent upon the UN fund raising $10 billion.

More significantly, as Friends of the Earth, Karen Orenstein, notes, "$3 billion falls magnitudes below what is actually needed by developing countries to confront a climate crisis that is not of their making."

Social movements and countries from the Global South have maintained over the years that rich countries owe a "climate debt" that should be paid in the form of reparations. At the COP16 in Cancún years ago, for example, developing countries and social movements had evaluated that the debt of developed countries to be an equivalent of $100 billion annually. As the nation that has economically benefited the most from the burning of fossil fuels, the U.S. is viewed as being responsible for a major portion of that amount.

Since then, this issue of who will pay for the ongoing human impacts of climate change has been central to climate change conferences and negotiations. While most of the emissions driving global warming come from wealthy nations, numerous studies show that poor nations across the world—which are also those who have contributed least to creating the crisis—face the greatest impact. Janet Redman, climate policy director at the Institute for Policy Studies, placed the issue in its true perspective when she stressed that "The impacts of climate change—extreme storms, water scarcity, food shortages—are no longer threats. For vulnerable communities around the world they are a reality."

The matter not only of responsibility but also of the financial wherewithal to meet this responsibility assumes further clarity when it is understood that the U.S. military, alone, spent $575 billion last year, much of that directed against the people of developing nations in the "War against Terror." These monies, of course, could have been put to better use by helping people in the Global South to deal with the impacts of the climate change that they didn't cause.

Adding insult to injury (and death), a report released by the Overseas Development Institute and Oil Change International found that G20 countries are collectively spending $88 billion a year in public funds to finance the fossil fuel industry's discovery of new gas, coal, and oil sources. This flies in the face of the world's desperate need to immediately reduce the burning of fossil fuels, thus casting the White House pledge of $3 billion in a very different light. Not only is the latter a drop in the bucket, it's also an instance of the "all of the above" shell game of Obama's energy policy. These lavish subsidies to the fossil fuel industry by the Global North only exacerbates the same climate change that is especially felt by the very countries toward whom his act of "generosity" is directed and supposedly intended to help.

A more complete picture of our government's true intentions toward the Global South is presented by former SIT (now NYU) professor, Christian Parenti in his excellent book, *Tropic of Chaos*. In it, he writes of the "catastrophic convergence" of political, economic, and environmental disasters that particularly effect "a belt of economically and politically battered postcolonial states girding the planet's mid-latitudes" between the Tropics of Capricorn and Cancer.

He points out how these countries are not only "heavily dependent on agriculture and fishing, thus very vulnerable to shifts in weather patterns," they were also "on the front lines of the Cold War and neoliberal economic restructuring." As such, they constitute "most of the failed and semi-failed states in the developing world." Home to some 2.7 billion people, these 46 countries are where "the current and impending dislocations of climate change intersect with the already existing crises of poverty and violence."

Within this context, Parenti sees a response from Washington and its European allies that are at sharp variance with Obama's $3 billion gift. He writes about *"the politics of the armed lifeboat,"* where "a green authoritarianism [is] emerging in rich countries, while the climate crisis pushes the Third World into chaos." Rather than addressing the root causes of this crisis, the Pentagon and its allies have for some time now been "actively planning a militarized adaptation, which emphasizes the long-term, open-ended containment of failed or failing states," what Parenti terms as "counterinsurgency forever."

This strategy, of course, has notably failed in the past, from Vietnam to Iraq and Afghanistan; even more importantly, it is "one of the historical streams leading into the catastrophic convergence," as Parenti underscores throughout his book. This "climate fascism, a politics based on exclusion, segregation, and repression" is a recipe for disaster, not only for the Global South, but for us in the Global North, as well. For as Parenti correctly points out, these countries "cannot collapse without eventually taking wealthy economies down with them. If climate change is allowed to destroy whole economies and nations, no amount of walls, guns, barbed wire, armed aerial drones, or permanently deployed mercenaries will be able to save one half of the planet from the other."

Just as social injustice is responsible for the world we've created, so, too, is social justice the heart of a sane and doable transition to a post-oil world. Values—not technology, and certainly not politics—are the key to any success. It's not so much what we do about the climate crisis (as important as that is!), as it is how we go about doing it. That's the missing link to a successful revolution.

CHAPTER 22

Hope Without Expectation

ARE we becoming a people without hope?

At the present time, Americans appear to be suffering from a paralysis of will when it comes to acting proactively on climate change. It's not that we are unaware of it, or that we refute its existence; to the contrary, we are concerned, and many of us are frankly disturbed by it.

Rather, as I wrote in the 14 August issue of the *Reformer*, it's a failure to integrate this awareness into our everyday lives and to transform it into social action. Knowledge does not seem to carry a moral imperative to act. What is disowned here is not the fact of climate change, but rather the psychological, political, and moral implications that one would expect to follow from such awareness, that would promote a daily practice of appropriate behaviors.

While there are many understandable reasons for this situation—feelings of powerlessness, fear of the future, incapacitating grief and guilt, ineffectual political leadership, the unprecedented nature of the climate challenge, to name some—the failure to do the right thing can perhaps be best understood as an absence of hope.

The Merriam-Webster Dictionary defines hope as "to want something to happen or be true, and think[ing] that it could happen or be true." While it doesn't guarantee anything, the presence of hope at least suggests the possibility of realizing the desired outcome. Our situation, that is, is not *hopeless*.

This standard definition, however, doesn't include two key elements which make hope real: intention and behavior. Such is their importance that their absence is fatal to maintaining a sense of reasonable hope in the face of climate change. The passive nature that the dictionary imparts to hope ignores the decisive role of human agency, of the importance of acting intentionally and proactively upon that which we hope to realize. Minus our active involvement, we have little reason to be hopeful.

In their book, *Active Hope,* Joanna Macy and Chris Johnstone write about the need for "becoming active participants in bringing about what we hope for." They observe that hope "is something we *do* rather than *have.*" This is in contrast to the more conventional understanding which asserts that we must first have hope in order to act. What this misleading notion fails to address, however, is where hope originates beyond simply wishful thinking. Macy and Johnstone correct this shortcoming by noting that "The guiding impetus is intention; we *choose* what we aim to bring about, act for, or express. Rather than weighing our chances and proceeding only when we feel hopeful, we focus on our intention and let it be our guide."

Intentionality means a commitment to action. We don't leave hope and its realization to chance. Instead, we demonstrate that they are dynamic partners by acting on our lives. Hope is a condition of living our lives in those ways that make possible a post-oil world in which we can both survive and thrive. When we do this, our hopes are congruent with an appropriate practice. Being an actor in our present lives is what justifies faith in the time ahead. Only a daily practice that proclaims our hope for the future can get us from here to there.

This understanding is amplified by Kate Davies. In her recent *Tikkun* op-ed piece, "Hope in the Age of Climate Consequences." Her stance supports the second element of real hope, ethical behavior. She writes about hope being "an orientation of the spirit," which she terms, "intrinsic hope," one that "emphasizes resilience and agency. It accepts whatever happens and does whatever needs to be done." The consequence is a daily practice whereby "we act because it is the loving and caring thing to do, rather than because we expect to succeed."

As Davies suggests, while essential, acting intentionally does not alone make us hopeful about our prospects to limit climate change. This only occurs when the focus of our daily behavior is upon living the values of a peaceful, socially just, sustainable world. Hope, in other words, is also a matter of how we go about doing what needs to be done. Only then, when process and goal are one, can we be reasonably optimistic about the possibilities for a peaceful, socially just, sustainable world.

The delicious irony, of course, is that by acting on our values for their own sake, we invariably create the propitious circumstances that allow us to be hopeful. Being proactive with our values inspires hope. In fact, at moments like this, it's really quite impossible to distinguish between the doing and being of hope. They seamlessly blend with one another as the unity they are.

Hope is possible when we act with selfless love, personal integrity, moral courage, and a basic commitment to the sacredness of life. Unfortunately, a values-based practice is not a regular or consistent part of our species' behavioral repertoire. Too often, we are prone to greed, violence, and self-aggrandizement. This is why we're in the fix we are today. Whether we choose to act upon our heart's values, or not, is crucial to the people we are and the world we live in. When we behave in ways necessary to create a viable post-oil world, we access these essential human values, along with the power and credibility they lend to our efforts.

At these moments, we come alive! We tap into our innate capacity for kindness, generosity, and compassion; for forgiveness, truth and love, as well as other qualities we prize. Because our behavior is informed by our heart's values, we do the right thing without expectations; in so doing, we find that our actions are their own reward.

CHAPTER 23

A Call for Climate Collaboration

ONE of the most unfortunate fates that can victimize activists is the failure to work together in a collaborative fashion to accomplish a common goal. At its worst, individuals and groups who are pursuing the same goal end up in an adversarial, even internecine, relationship, frequently over what appear to be the most trivial differences, which really come down to ego posturing. Not only are we shooting ourselves in the foot at these times, and rendering null any chance of success, to an outside observer it appears that what or whom we're really opposing is one another!

Though fortunately not as extreme, the movement toward a habitable world beyond fossil fuels nevertheless has been divided between two approaches that at an earlier time were known as adaptation and mitigation and are now called resilience and resistance. On the one hand, there are those who correctly believe that we need to build sustainable, resilient communities if we are to successfully transition into the post-petroleum world toward which we are moving. On the other hand, there are those who are equally right in their assertion that we have to create a grassroots political presence that will convince politicians and Big Oil alike to adopt policies that will reduce greatly our carbon emissions so as to avoid climate catastrophe.

But while this division might have been a workable arrangement at an earlier time, especially as both approaches are equally valid, we have now reached the point where it is a luxury we can ill afford. Times have changed as reflected by the fact that words like "adaptation" and "mitigation" have been replaced by the more appropriately urgent phrases, "resilience" and "resistance."

This is graphically underscored by three, basic facts about our present situation. One: we must leave eighty percent of the proven coal, oil, and gas reserves in the ground if we are to have any chance of preventing global temperatures from rising more than 2° Celsius and beyond, which the scientific community believes we must do if we are to avoid climate disaster. Two: Big Oil is giving no indication that it is backing away from the trillions of dollars of potential profits that it feels it can realize by going after the remaining fossil fuels, but rather is engaged in a frenzied black-gold rush, as evidenced by the billions of dollars that it's currently investing in the exploration and extraction of unconventional fuels (tar sands, heavy oil, hydrofracked gas and oil), as well as coal mining and (very) deep-ocean drilling. And three, as we read almost daily, climate change is occurring at the "fastest pace since the age of dinosaurs." With only a .8-degree rise in temperature, for example, the East Antarctic ice, previously "thought to be at little risk from climate change," is melting; heat waves are "inevitable in the century ahead"; the acidification of the oceans is occurring "at a rate unseen in 250,000 years"; and the calamitous, "hundred- (or thousand-) year" weather events are routinely afflicting our world.

In this world, adhering to more limiting, one-sided visions of what needs to be done has become a liability for all concerned. The bar has been raised from preparing for the world that our grandchildren will inherit to dealing with the one we live in right now. Time is running out. It is critical that both the resilience and resistance sides understand that we need each other to build a larger, more effective movement if we are to realize the post-petroleum society that both sides want. We need to come together under a common understanding that if we don't stop Big Oil from its mindless pursuit of the last drop in the ground, the question of sustainable communities is moot, and unless we re-localize ourselves and become a resilient, self- and community-sufficient people who can increasingly live successfully without oil, we won't be able to roll with the unprecedented and uniquely challenging world that we will experience increasingly in the years ahead, even if we turn off the fossil-fuel spigot today.

Just as people, in general, need to behave as if climate change is real, and to translate their awareness into concrete measures in their everyday lives, so too do activists—as represented most notably by 350.org and Transition Town folks—need to extend themselves. While continuing with the good work they're presently doing separately to build resilience and resistance, they need to move beyond the comfort zones of familiar activist paradigms, and become more involved with one another. We must reach out to one another to explore how we can work together, perhaps arriving at a collaborative model that will enhance our opportunities for success against the odds we presently face. By so doing, we will create a larger, more viable presence in our communities to represent what needs to be done, and how it can be accomplished, providing a visible example of people who work together, peacefully and cooperatively, united by a common effort.

One of the factors that can greatly assist this process is the growing appreciation on the part of all concerned of the values that we share. Ours is not an adversarial movement, despite our need to discover ways to transition away from fossil fuels. We are not interested in exerting power over others, or in controlling the world. We recognize that this is precisely the paradox that lies at the root of our dilemma today. Ours is a movement that must embrace all members of society, including those with whom we disagree, for we believe that in order to transition successfully to avoid the climate crisis we face, all members of our communities must be involved.

However, when we encounter forces that, by their actions, threaten our very existence, as we do today with Big Oil, we must resist them. We can do this by engaging them in direct, nonviolent, principled ways. We must resist the efforts of those who endanger our lives, but we must refrain from destructive behavior.

Finally, it is such shared values as participatory democracy, social justice, and compassion toward all living beings that are particularly important in the behavior of activists, successfully engaging our neighbors. For in the case of building both resilience and resistance, the ultimate issue is that of an involved, empowered citizenry, the everyday man and woman who are participants in a grassroots movement to reverse the power balance in the halls of government and to build increasingly sustainable, resilient communities. This is what ultimately will stop Big Oil, and will make possible a successful transition to a post-oil world. In fact, it is the only thing that will.

CHAPTER 24

We Can Do It.
But Will We?

THE climate news for October, 2014 was most discouraging, especially coming as it did on the heels of the inspiring Peoples Climate March in New York City at the end of September.

The month's depressing lowlights included the announcement by NASA that August was the hottest month globally since records began to be kept in 1880. This was followed shortly thereafter with an update that September was now the hottest month ever, and that 2014 was right on track to become the hottest year on record. And as if this wasn't enough, carbon emissions continued to increase, rising this year to record levels.

All of this assumed more alarming proportions when a study published in *New Scientist* found that scientists have greatly underestimated the extent of global warming because temperature readings from the southern hemisphere oceans were inaccurate. "One could say that global warming is ocean warming," noted two authors of the study from the US National Oceanic and Atmospheric Administration. "Quantifying how fast and where the ocean is warming is vital to understanding how much and how fast the atmosphere will warm, and seas will rise." This discovery meant that the world is warming faster than we thought.

But arguably the most disheartening news was the report from the World Wildlife Federation that the Earth's vertebrate wildlife populations have halved over the past 40 years because of biodiversity loss. Specifically, there are now 52 percent less mammals, fish, birds, reptiles, and amphibians than there were in 1974. As Professor Ken Norris, director at the Zoological Society of London, observed, "The scale of biodiversity loss has reached critical levels, and damage to the very ecosystems that are essential to our existence is alarming. The damage is a consequence of the way we choose to live."

At a time when scientists are increasingly warning that, "We have five minutes before midnight" (Rajendra Pachauri, head of the United Nations Intergovernmental Panel on Climate Change), and that we're in the "Zero Decade" and must get it right very soon if we are to have any chance of avoiding catastrophic and irreversible climate change, October was not reassuring.

It's not a question of what we can do: there are many things we could do, even now, at this 11+[th] hour, to avert climate catastrophe. As we demonstrated with the Marshall Plan after World War II, and the Apollo effort to put a human being on the moon, we're capable of harnessing the financial and technological resources required to undertake enormous projects. Nothing less than a similar effort must be initiated for the climate, right now.

Rather, the question is, are we as a people willing to do what needs to be done to avoid a global crisis that threatens societal collapse and species extinction?

Are we capable of making the necessary sacrifices around our consumerist way of life for the sake of our children and grandchildren, not to mention the remaining half of the vertebrate population, as well?

Can we act this selflessly?

And what exactly needs to be done? Solar panels and cargo bikes, community gardens and farmers markets are commendable; but obviously they and other individual lifestyle changes have no measurable effect on the system change we need to make in our burning of fossil fuels.

In his now classic article for *Rolling Stone,* "Global Warming's Terrifying New Math," Bill McKibben pointed out that in order to have any chance of keeping global temperatures below 2° Centigrade, which has been generally agreed as the red line that we can't cross (we're currently at .9°), we could "safely" burn only 565 of the 2795 gigatons of carbon already contained in the proven coal, oil and gas reserves in the ground. In short, we'd have to keep 80 percent of those reserves locked away underground to avoid disaster.

What this means is that the big oil companies have to walk away from the billions of potential profits represented by that 80 percent that would remain in the ground. Whatever else they do, like converting to renewable energy companies, they can no longer be fossil fuel companies. They have to put the rest of life before their bottom line, instead.

It also means that, at least for those of us who have enjoyed the material abundance afforded by the age of oil during the last 150 years, we will have to accept a much more modest lifestyle. (No, there is no green version of the fossil fuel economy, which is based on the continued extraction of finite resources to feed the insatiable appetite of infinite growth.) Quite simply, we're going to have to give up the kind of life we now take for granted.

But more yet, if we're to survive climate change, we as a species must move beyond the insufferable hubris that we've exhibited toward the rest of life for 10,000 years that began with the dawn of agriculture, and accelerated exponentially with the so-called "Enlightenment" (Francis Bacon's declaration that "Nature can be conquered"), the Industrial Revolution and the discovery of fossil fuels. This is the defining characteristic of Western Civilization, an approach and attitude that views us as both independent of, as well as superior to, the rest of nature. It is this original power relationship—humans over the rest of life—

that has allowed us to oppress, abuse, exploit, and otherwise visit upon other living beings, including our own kind, the violence of mindlessness—the rule of heartlessness—as if they were not an integral part in the web of life. This must change as well.

As daunting as all of this may appear to be in the context of the times we live, this challenge also represents an unprecedented opportunity for our species to finally get it right. Necessity could be the midwife of virtue in this instance, simply because, if we want to realize a successful transition to a sane and viable post-oil world, we have no choice but to be the truly enlightened, civilized species we've always claimed to be. This is our no-choice moment. As much as climate change is about changing the source of our energy, it is even more about changing the values we choose to live by. Moral courage, personal integrity, and selfless love, all of which we've demonstrated a capacity for at moments throughout our history, need to now be practiced with an everyday constancy, supplanting the greed, violence, self-aggrandizement, and disrespect for the sacredness of life that has led us to our present dilemma.

Can we do this? Of course we can. It's just a question of whether we will.

EPILOGUE:

A Revolution
of Everyday Life

WHY do revolutions invariably fail as revolutions, including (especially) those that come to power?

More importantly, perhaps, what is the relevance of such a question to building resilient, adaptable communities for a post-oil age, ones that can sustain their members in the context of the unprecedented climate change that is increasingly influencing our world?

The answer to the first question is that, rather than creating the liberating alternative their slogans and rhetoric promise, revolutions are invariably little more than a "revolutionary" variation of the oppressive arrangement they're replacing, the overthrow of one power arrangement with another. That's their fatal flaw: the inability to translate their expressed goal of human liberation into an actual revolution of everyday life.

As for the second question, revolution is germane to a successful transition to a post-oil world: if we're to accomplish a sustainable existence, then we'll have to be the peaceful, socially just, collaborative people that revolution calls for and that resilient communities require for the unprecedented transformation we will be making. The millennia-long, species-specific struggle to dominate and control nature and each other is at the heart of the climate crisis. It is crystal clear from all that we're witnessing at present in our economic, political, social, and cultural worlds that this no longer works, that our way of life is coming apart, and that we can no longer continue doing business as usual and expecting to survive at the same time. It's time to move forward.

What the history of revolution has to teach us is that, rather than finally supplanting the ancient hierarchy of one-up over one-down by acting as examples of an enlightened alternative, humans typically have opted instead for a "revolutionary" version of the power-over dynamic—oppressed over oppressor—as the transitional stage between the status quo and the revolutionary goal.

Within the context of our violent, predatory, often unconscionable world of power-politics that makes revolution necessary in the first place, this has seemed to make sense. After all, the issue that is being addressed is one of power and, specifically, its distribution: who has it, and who does not. This is why people have long believed that a fundamental change in human relationships cannot be accomplished without first achieving a political settlement that removes the oppressor from power and replaces it with a rule of the oppressed. Only then, with this necessary change in the power dynamic that allows for the new politically-correct order to be enacted, is a revolution of everyday life possible. Only then, have we believed, can the ideals of revolution have a chance to prevail, to become reality.

By pursuing human liberation through power-struggles, however, revolution replicates the original conditions of force and violence, domination and control. This is so even if, this time, it's the "good guys" who triumph over the "bad guys."

For while revolution and the transition to a post-petroleum world are both questions of power, they are not ones of political power, and its domination/submission dynamic that is at its core. A one-up/one-down arrangement poisons the integrity of any relationship we could rightly term "revolutionary," precluding as it does the compassion, forgiveness, and reconciliation that are so crucial to a truly revolutionary relationship. In so doing, revolution becomes counter revolutionary, corrupting and distorting the ideals of "Liberté, Égalité, Fraternité," negating the salutary, transformative potential of the human spirit to which, at its best, revolution speaks.

By viewing our situation in political terms, we only obscure what is really at issue here, for both revolution and a post-oil transition: the business of empowering ourselves. Taking responsibility for our wellbeing and acting responsibly for the wellbeing of other living beings is the missing link between where we are and where we want to be. This is the connection that allows revolution and a sustainable transition to a post-oil world to be one, providing us with the necessary power to successfully transition to the new world we're entering. It is only when we act on our lives as best we can, living them in accordance with our values, that we possess the requisite power to transition to a post-petroleum world in which we can both survive and thrive.

Despite their daunting nature, what is especially propitious about our present circumstances is that they don't allow us the luxury of that uniquely human capacity for putting off until tomorrow what needs to be done today. Having run out of time, we must act now as a matter of necessity. We can no longer afford to postpone the revolution in human relationships that lies at the heart of a successful transition. There is nothing we need to accomplish first before we do what we're always telling ourselves we should be doing. Living at the dawn of a post-oil world, with climate change proceeding more rapidly than scientists thought possible, we have no other choice than to embrace a revolution of everyday life by actually living the values of such an existence. We just need to do it!